STRATEGIC ARMS REDUCTIONS

Michael M. May
George F. Bing
John D. Steinbruner

*Prepared in cooperation with
the Lawrence Livermore National Laboratory*

The Brookings Institution
Washington, D.C.

Copyright © 1988 by

THE BROOKINGS INSTITUTION

1775 Massachusetts Avenue, N.W., Washington, D.C. 20036

Library of Congress Cataloging-in-Publication Data

May, Michael M., 1925–
    Strategic arms reductions.

    1. Nuclear warfare.   2. Strategic forces—United
States.   3. Strategic forces—Soviet Union.   4. Nuclear
arms control.   5. Deterrence (Strategy)   I. Bing,
George F., 1924–   .   II. Steinbruner, John D.,
1941–   .   III. Title.
U263.M345   1988   355'.0217   88-16901
ISBN 0-8157-5525-2 (pbk.)

9 8 7 6 5 4 3 2 1

Foreword

By popular standards of common sense the nuclear arsenals of the United States and the Soviet Union have long seemed excessive, and in recent years the two governments themselves have implicitly endorsed this perspective. A substantial reduction has become an explicit goal for both sides and appears to be a likely event.

That prospect raises a basic question: what level of nuclear weapons deployment is appropriate to support the central purpose of preventing war? It is a question not readily answered at the moment either by common judgment or by government staff work. Negotiations have focused on a figure of 6,000 strategic warheads as an immediate objective but have not yet developed a clear rationale for that figure as compared with the many others that might be considered plausible. As the reduction of strategic forces becomes practical, more precise thinking about the outcome will certainly be necessary.

In 1980 the U.S. National Academy of Sciences established the Committee on International Security and Arms Control to discuss security issues with professional colleagues in the Soviet Union. In the course of these discussions, possible strategic arms reductions were considered and standard calculations of physical weapons effects were used to assess the significance of these reductions. The immediate purpose was to define areas of technical agreement as a means of identifying the important differences in individual and national perspective.

The analysis presented in this study evolved from those discussions. It too is designed to promote public reflection and does not attempt to settle with any precision the eternal question of how much is enough. It does specify different ways in which strategic forces might be reduced, and in comparing their effects, it identifies some of the important judgments that must be made. The study was done in cooperation with the Lawrence Livermore National Laboratory.

Michael M. May is associate director at large and George F. Bing is a staff scientist at the Lawrence Livermore National Laboratory. John D. Steinbruner is director of Foreign Policy Studies at Brookings. The authors wish to thank the many people who have contributed to the project. Lew Allen, Jr., Solomon Buchsbaum, Albert Clogston, Paul Doty, Herman Feshbach, Alexander Flax, Edward Frieman, Richard Garwin, Alexander George, Marvin Goldberger, David Hamburg, Spurgeon Keeney, Jr., Catherine Kelleher, Joshua Lederberg, Claire Max, Richard A. Muller, Wolfgang Panofsky, Frank Press, Victor Rabinowitch, Marshall Rosenbluth, Malvin Ruderman, Lynn Rusten, Charles Townes, and Jerome Wiesner participated in the discussions that inspired the study and made comments on early drafts. Lieutenant Colonel Richard Wittler, U.S. Air Force, helped develop the computer analysis done at the Livermore Laboratory. At the Brookings Institution, Lisa Mages provided research assistance, and Daniel A. Lindley III and Amy Waychoff verified the manuscript. Karen Kimball at the Livermore Laboratory and Kathryn Ho at Brookings handled the details of preparing the manuscript. Jeanette Morrison edited the text.

Financial support for the study was provided through the Brookings Institution by the Carnegie Corporation of New York and by the John D. and Catherine T. MacArthur Foundation, and through the Lawrence Livermore National Laboratory by the U.S. Department of Energy. That support is gratefully acknowledged.

The views expressed are those of the authors and should not be ascribed to the persons or organizations whose assistance is acknowledged or to the trustees, officers, or other staff members of the Brookings Institution, the Lawrence Livermore National Laboratory, or the National Academy of Sciences.

BRUCE A. MACLAURY
President

April 1988
Washington, D.C.

Contents

Tables

Figures

Strategic Arms Reductions

ONE

Introduction

The idea of the United States and the Soviet Union reducing their offensive strategic forces by 50 percent or more, once considered radically impractical, has in recent years become a respectable, feasible prospect. Reductions of this size have been outlined in formal negotiations, and an agreement could probably be reached were the dispute over the Antiballistic Missile Treaty to be resolved. Anticipation of this result reflects the emergence of a widely shared practical assessment that the capacities of the opposing nuclear arsenals exceed the requirements of deterrence and that equitable reductions would improve international security.

There are reasonable grounds for these presumptions, but they have not yet achieved either the precision or the degree of consensus necessary for carrying out an agreed reduction of strategic forces. The demands of such an agreement would reach well beyond the precedent now being set by the projected removal of intermediate-range nuclear missiles from Europe. Not only would active weapons have to be destroyed and at least some of their organizational units dismantled, but the technical design and operational configuration of the remaining

1

forces would probably have to be substantially adjusted as well. Since these adjustments affect the core of the U.S. and Soviet military establishments, they would inevitably evoke differences in conceptual perspective, organizational interest, political commitment, and other basic matters that influence policy decisions. To produce a coherent result, policymakers will need to evolve a more refined understanding of the exact purpose and design of strategic force reductions. Extensive public discussion will undoubtedly accompany this process in the United States.

We hope to facilitate this discussion by reviewing technical facts and strategic principles that appear to provide the basis for consensus. Our intention is to examine these factors in detail, though they may seem obvious to some, to see whether they support the policy preferences and strategic preconceptions associated with deep cuts in strategic forces.

The overarching purpose of offensive strategic weapons is not disputed: they are universally meant to prevent war by presenting a deterrent threat. As this principle has been translated into specific target assignments, however, dilemmas and differences in judgment have emerged about three basic missions that current strategic forces prepare to perform. These missions involve attacks on, respectively, strategic weapons, military infrastructure, and critical industrial capability.

The first, the counterstrategic mission, is an acknowledged source of danger to any deterrent arrangement. To the extent that it succeeds, an attack on the opponent's strategic weapons would reduce the destructive potential arrayed against one's own society but would also thereby diminish the opponent's deterrent capability. Today and under reasonable technical projections for the future, the expected success of such first-strike attacks is too partial and uncertain to provide a rational motive for initiating war, but under intense crisis circumstances the chance of even partial success might be enough to trigger an uncontrollable interaction. The first-strike mission against strategic weapons cannot be rationalized as an effective policy by either side, but it is sufficiently feared as a possible policy of the opponent to be a significant practical problem. Any acceptable arms reduction arrangement certainly must not enhance this mission and probably should diminish it. Indeed, limiting the threat to strategic weapons and thus dampening the inclination to initiate war under crisis pressure seems to be a principal benefit that might be achieved by strategic force reductions, with appropriate constraints on the characteristics of the forces.

The second basic mission of offensive strategic arms is to attack the other forces and general infrastructure, nuclear and conventional, of the opponent—the assets that give coherence and direction to military power. These targets are the primary focus of the theory of deterrence that prevails within both the U.S. and Soviet military establishments, so far as we know. For one thing, nuclear weapons would be highly effective against these targets. For another, they can be meaningfully attacked in a retaliatory strike. Thus the professional military judge this mission to be both a credible and a persuasive deterrent threat— and also a mission that should be exercised in retaliation if every dimension of "victory" is to be denied an attacker.

In contrast, the third kind of strategic mission, which targets the opponent's critical industrial capability, is directed less against its immediate military capability than against its calculus of national objectives. Exercise of this mission against industrial targets would inevitably lead to massive casualties in nearby populations. This mission reflects the criterion of deterrence most prominently mentioned—and debated—in political discussions of the subject. It rests on the fact that large proportions of the industrial facilities and the nearby urban populations of both the United States and the Soviet Union could be readily destroyed in a retaliatory strike with a relatively small number of weapons. Some believe this fact provides an adequate basis for deterrence at the lowest level of forces, while others, finding social destruction to be immoral and insufficiently credible, implicitly side with the more demanding military conception. There is a substantial range of opinion in the United States about the basic requirements that reduced strategic forces must be able to meet.

The obvious question, then, is whether a level and configuration of strategic forces can be defined that would restrict the ability of either side to attack strategic weapons while preserving the capacity to retaliate against either military infrastructure or industrial facilities or both. This result could at least potentially command the broad consensus needed to implement it. It would diminish the counterstrategic mission that is feared as a potential source of unmanageable crisis pressures. And it would not require a decisive resolution of the U.S. domestic disagreement over the appropriate focus of retaliation, general military assets or industry and populations.

It is also important to ask whether such an outcome can be accomplished with the current division of forces into submarine, bomber, and land-based missile components. Preserving the basic organizational structure of strategic forces would minimize the process of adjustment.

Technical assessments cannot provide undisputed answers to these questions, but they can provide useful definition and a partial framework for judgment. With that in mind, we have considered the effects of strategic force reductions using the standard parameters of weapons performance: the number and yield of warheads, and the alert rate, operational reliability, accuracy, and susceptibility to blast damage of delivery systems. We have looked at six potential configurations of strategic forces for the United States and the Soviet Union, three each at levels of 6,000 and 3,000 warheads. Details of our force models are given in section 2. We have compared the expected performance of these reduced strategic forces with that of current forces using two complementary methods of analysis. The first assesses the extent to which each side can expect to destroy the opponent's strategic forces in a surprise first strike. The assumptions and results of this analysis are presented in section 3, Drawdown of Forces. The second and more detailed method assesses the outcome of strategic force exchanges between the two sides. The measures of performance are the ability of the forces to attack the target systems of the other side, both in first strike and in retaliation, and the ability to maintain reserves of about 10 percent for later contingencies. These analyses are discussed in section 4, Exchange Calculations. We have also assessed in approximate terms the immediate human fatalities that would be expected to result from these force exchanges. Details of these calculations are provided in section 5, Civil Damage.

For the 6,000-warhead configurations, these analyses were purposely biased against the retaliating force to pose a test of deterrent capability that was severe to the point of being unrealistic: we assumed that the country initiating attack would have all its strategic assets immediately available, while the victim would be unwarned and would have only those on normal or day-to-day alert. For the 3,000-warhead force configurations, this disparity in readiness was reduced on the assumption that these lower force levels would be accompanied by greater investment in measures to provide higher sustainable alert rates and more rapid response to warning.

The results of these assessments are subject to all the doubt and variation in interpretation that arise from partial, uncertain calculations. They do, nonetheless, support a number of observations that set useful terms for discussion:

—At present levels of forces (about 10,000 strategic warheads on each side), mutual deterrence is assured without too fine a reckoning of the details of the forces or how they might be used. The most successful hypothetical surprise attack by either side would still leave the other with more than 3,000 effective strategic nuclear weapons, assuming that submarines at sea survive and that the command systems are able to perform their functions.

—There is a practical limit, though it has yet to be authoritatively determined, to the number of targets, other than fixed missile sites, the attacked side must be able to strike in retaliation under even the most demanding concept of deterrence. A plausible upper bound appears to be 1,500–2,000 targets, beyond which the marginal contribution to the overall effect would be so small that a prudent military command would presumably choose to preserve any remaining weapons rather than to expend them in redundant and unnecessary retaliation.

—Within the bounds of this plausible deterrent requirement, the threat to human life and society is only modestly affected, if at all, by differences in targeting policy. Attacks on military infrastructure and critical military industries involving large numbers of weapons would do roughly as much civilian damage as smaller attacks focusing directly and exclusively on urban-industrial targets.

—Any of the 6,000-warhead force configurations investigated could readily strike 1,500–2,000 targets in retaliation and thus meet the basic deterrent requirement. At the 6,000-warhead level, the major difference between forces configured to preserve or increase the ability to attack the other side's strategic weapons (for example, when both sides emphasize accurate, high-yield MIRVed missile weapons) and those configured primarily for survivability (with both sides emphasizing mobile missiles and submarines) is in the balance of forces remaining after an exchange. In the former case, emphasizing counterforce capability, the side striking first would have a substantial advantage in residual forces after an exchange. In the latter case, emphasizing survivability, the disparity in residual forces would be eliminated. Since both sides' military organizations would be damaged beyond immediate repair in the course of the initial attack and the retaliation, any disparity in residual forces would be of questionable practical significance, although it probably would affect formal negotiations and might affect later force structure design.

—At 3,000 warheads, strategic force deployments would be set very close to the plausible upper bound for the deterrent requirement, and configurations of force that increase survivability would matter much more. Neither side could carry out a preemptive attack on the opponent's strategic forces without reducing the available weapons needed to threaten the basic deterrent target set. Neither side would have the protection against such a preemptive attack that the sheer number of available weapons currently provides. Such a tailoring of the strategic balance would presumably be attractive to those who believe that mutual regulation is a desirable and feasible basis for international security. It would be less comfortable to those who prefer to maintain security on more unilateral terms and who discount the problem of uncontrollable force interaction.

—Civilian damage, measured in deaths, does not appear very sensitive to levels of strategic forces. This result is due mainly to the assumption that high-priority targets are located near or in populated areas, an assumption that seems realistic. The number of deaths does depend on the yield of the weapons used, as might be expected. The yield needed to destroy a military target collocated with a populated area is smaller than the yields generally assumed to be available to the two strategic forces. Reducing yield would be desirable on this count. An agreement to this effect would be difficult or impossible to verify, but verification may not be critical, since military usefulness does not vary rapidly with yield. Yield reduction could be a desirable unilateral measure.

TWO

The Force Models

A principal objective of this study is to make quantitative assessments of the capabilities of reduced strategic forces. The first step is to specify the composition and characteristics of the several hypothesized reduced forces. These force "models," as well as current U.S. and Soviet hypothesized forces, are summarized in this section. Much of our assessment is based on comparing estimated capabilities of the reduced-force models with those estimated for current forces.

The current forces are assumed to have about 10,000 strategic nuclear warheads on each side. Reduced forces are considered at levels of 6,000, because it is the lowest figure seriously suggested by either side, and 3,000, to explore the consequences of deeper cuts.

We did not look below 3,000 warheads because we believe that figure is at or close to the limits of validity of our methods and assumptions. Below about 3,000 a number of new assumptions regarding, for instance, disposition of noncentral and of allied nuclear forces, direction of arms control policies, targeting policy, and so forth, would have to be made if the analysis carried out here is to retain even the modest degree of relevance to policy that it may have at the higher levels.

Table 1 for the United States and table 2 for the Soviet Union summarize the force structures. The current, or "baseline," forces are adapted from the standard unclassified tabulations that appear regularly in *Soviet Military Power, The Military Balance,* and other sources.[1]

The baseline force data are as of early 1986 and thus do not include, for example, more recent deployments of the MX missile and the B-1 bomber. For the United States, we have assumed 180 B-52 bombers, each armed with 12 warheads, either cruise missiles or a mixture of bombs and SRAMs (short-range attack missiles). These numbers are adapted from *The Military Balance 1985-1986*. Other sources give larger B-52 inventories and suggest higher weapon loads. We believe the cited values are a good approximation to actual day-to-day heavy bomber forces. Neither U.S. nor Soviet medium bombers have been included in our analysis. U.S. FB-111s with 6 warheads each would account for about 15 percent of all U.S. bomber warheads and provide about 2 percent of all strategic warheads on day-to-day alert.

We consider six structures for the reduced forces, labeled A through F. Cases A, B, and C posit 6,000 warheads on each side, and cases D, E, and F, 3,000. The weapon systems included in the hypothesized reduced forces are all either currently deployed or well defined and soon to be deployed. The important characteristics of the reduced-force cases are as follows:

Case A (Proportionally reduced forces, 6,000 warheads). Forces

---

1. U.S. Department of Defense, *Soviet Military Power 1986* and earlier editions (Washington, D.C.: Government Printing Office, 1986); International Institute for Strategic Studies, *The Military Balance 1985–1986* (London: IISS, 1985); Department of Defense, Joint Chiefs of Staff, *United States Military Posture FY 1987* (Washington, D.C.: JCS, 1986), p. 19; U.S. Congress, Congressional Budget Office, *Modernizing U.S. Strategic Offensive Forces: The Administration's Program and Alternatives* (GPO, 1983); Thomas B. Cochran, William M. Arkin, and Milton M. Hoenig, *Nuclear Weapons Databook,* vol. 1: *U.S. Nuclear Forces and Capabilities* (Ballinger, 1984); and U.S. Arms Control and Disarmament Agency, *Arms Control and Disarmament Agreements: Texts and Histories of Negotiations,* 1982 ed. (GPO, 1982).

TABLE 1. **Strategic force models for the United States**

| | Current forces, baseline | | 6,000 warheads | | | | | | 3,000 warheads | | | | | |
| | | | Case A | | Case B | | Case C | | Case D | | Case E | | Case F | |
System	Launchers (L)	Warheads (W)	L	W	L	W	L	W	L	W	L	W	L	W
Minuteman 2	450	450	250	250	...	...	...	...	250	250	...	...	...	...
Minuteman 3	250	750	...	...	...	...	...	...	...	...	...	...	...	...
Minuteman 3A	300	900	250	750	...	...	...	...	...	...	...	...	...	...
MX	...	...	...	...	1,000	1,000	50	500	...	...	...	...	50	500
Small ICBM	...	...	...	...	...	...	500	500	...	...	1,000	1,000	500	500
ICBM total	1,000	2,100	500	1,000	1,000	1,000	550	1,000	250	250	1,000	1,000	550	1,000
Silo total	1,000	...	500	...	0	...	50	...	250	...	0	...	50	...
Poseidon C-3	288	2,880	144	1,440	...	...	...	...	32	320	...	...	...	...
Poseidon/Trident C-4	360	2,880	192	1,536	360	2,880	...	...	192	1,536	192	1,536	...	...
Trident D-5	...	...	...	...	...	...	360	2,880	...	...	...	...	192	1,536
SLBM total	648	5,760	336	2,976	360	2,880	360	2,880	224	1,856	192	1,536	192	1,536
Submarines	37	...	17	...	15	...	15	...	10	...	8	...	8	...
B-52	180	2,160	...	...	...	...	...	...	...	...	...	...	...	...
B-1	...	...	101	2,020	106	2,120	106	2,120	45	900	47[a]	470	48[a]	480
Bomber total	180	2,160	101	2,020	106	2,120	106	2,120	45	900	47	470	48	480
Force totals	1,828	10,020	937	5,996	1,466	6,000	1,016	6,000	519	3,006	1,239	3,006	790	3,016

Sources: See text note 1.
a. Assumes only ten cruise missiles per bomber for these cases only.

TABLE 2. **Strategic force models for the Soviet Union**

System	Current forces, baseline		6,000 warheads						3,000 warheads					
	Launchers (L)	Warheads (W)	Case A		Case B		Case C		Case D		Case E		Case F	
			L	W	L	W	L	W	L	W	L	W	L	W
SS-11	448	448	200	200	...	...	...	...	...	...	...	...	...	...
SS-13	60	60	...	...	...	...	...	...	...	...	...	...	...	...
SS-17	150	600	100	400	...	...	...	...	...	...	...	...	...	...
SS-18	308	3,080	156	1,560	180	1,080	100	1,000	146	1,460	...	...	50	500
SS-19	360	2,160	180	1,080	990	990	1,000	1,000	...	...	1,000	1,000	...	...
SS-25	70	70	90	90	...	...	...	...	...	...	...	...	500	500
ICBM total	1,396	6,418	726	3,330	1,170	2,070	1,100	2,000	146	1,460	1,000	1,000	550	1,000
Silo total	1,326	...	636	...	180	...	100	...	146	...	0	...	50	...
SS-N-6	304	304	...	...	...	...	...	...	...	...	...	...	...	...
SS-N-8	292	292	...	...	...	...	...	...	...	...	...	...	...	...
SS-N-17	12	12	...	...	...	...	...	...	...	...	...	...	...	...
SS-N-18	224	1,568	160	1,120	...	...	...	...	...	...	...	...	...	...
SS-N-20	80	640	80	640	80	640	80	640	80	640	80	640	80	640
SS-N-23	32	256	80	640	272	2,176	272	2,176	80	640	96	768	112	895
SLBM total	944	3,072	320	2,400	352	2,816	352	2,816	160	1,280	176	1,408	192	1,535
Submarines	64	...	19	...	21	...	21	...	9	...	10	...	11	...
Bear	110	220	...	...	...	...	...	...	...	...	...	...	...	...
Bear H	40	160	66	264	...	...	...	...	66	264	...	...	...	...
Bison	30	120	...	...	...	...	...	...	...	...	...	...	...	...
Blackjack	...	...	...	...	55	1,100	60	1,200	...	...	60[a]	600	48[a]	480
Bomber total	180	500	66	264	55	1,100	60	1,200	66	264	60	600	48	480
Force totals	2,520	9,990	1,112	5,994	1,577	5,986	1,512	6,016	372	3,004	1,236	3,008	790	3,016

Sources: See text note 1.
a. Assumes only ten cruise missiles per bomber for these cases only.

similar in relative composition to the current forces except for the replacement of U.S. B-52s by B-1s.

Case B (Maximum mobility forces, 6,000 warheads). Forces selected for high survivability with a large proportion of mobile ICBMs and submarines. Few hard-target weapons are included.

Case C (Modernized forces, 6,000 warheads). A modernized force with an equal mix of silo-based and mobile ICBM warheads of high accuracy for each side. The United States has 360 Trident D-5s and 106 B-1 bombers.

Case D (Proportionally reduced forces, 3,000 warheads). An approximately proportional reduction of the forces of case A to a level of 3,000 warheads.

Case E (Maximum mobility forces, 3,000 warheads). A force emphasizing survivable elements, similar to case B. All land-based missiles are mobile.

Case F (Modernized forces, 3,000 warheads). A combination of modernized forces similar to case C.

Additional information about the assumed characteristics of the U.S. and Soviet weapon systems (for example, yields, accuracies, reliabilities, and alert rates) is presented in sections 3 and 4.

THREE

Drawdown of Forces

Today most analysts agree that neither the United States nor the Soviet Union is capable of a fully disarming first strike. Both countries have paid great attention to ensuring that a substantial fraction of their strategic forces would survive an initial exchange. Each side, knowing its offensive capabilities could not overwhelm the other's survival measures, believes that, even if it strikes first, it must still expect great destruction in retaliation.

In a severe crisis, however, if one or both sides believed a strategic nuclear war imminent and inevitable, a preemptive first strike might be judged the better choice compared with striking second, despite the consequences of retaliation. For maximum crisis stability, therefore, strategic forces should be designed, based, and operated in ways that minimize the incentives to such preemption. In this section we look at the baseline and the six hypothetical reduced-force models to see how they measure up.

A simple graphic way to consider the stability characteristics of two opposing forces is with "drawdown" curves. We have used them to show the results of U.S. and Soviet first strikes against the opposing superpower's warhead carriers. The starting point of each curve ("initial forces") is the total number of strategic warheads each side has before the strike. The final point is the remaining unused warheads of the attacker, and the surviving warheads of the side attacked before any attempt at retaliation. Intermediate segments of the curve show the drawdown, or reduction, of the important components of the force attacked (ballistic missile submarines in port, airfields with non-alert bombers, ICBMs in silos). The slope of the curve for a particular segment representing a force component is determined by the "exchange ratio" for that component. For example, a naval port with a submarine capable of carrying 160 warheads might be attacked by 4 warheads (to give high confidence of destroying the submarine); this would be an exchange ratio of 40 to 1. The ratio could be even higher if several submarines were in port.[2] A silo containing a MIRVed missile with 10 warheads attacked by two reliable, accurate missiles gives an exchange ratio of 5 to 1, while a silo containing a single-warhead missile (for example, a Minuteman 2) attacked by 2 warheads gives a ratio of 1 to 2.

Figures 2 through 8 are drawdown curves for the current U.S. and Soviet strategic forces and for the six assumed reduced-force cases in tables 1 and 2. Each figure has two drawdown curves: one for a Soviet first strike and one for a U.S. first strike.[3] The drawdown curves are not based on extensive calculations but follow straightforwardly from a set of assumptions we have made about the forces of each side. Assumptions are required about the alert posture and effectiveness of the forces striking first, and about the alert posture and vulnerabilities to attack of the various components of the side attacked. Our assumptions are listed in figure 1.

2. We have assumed for the purposes of this analysis that the submarine force, reflecting its traditions, would not be operationally configured for launch on warning and therefore not prepared to fire missiles from port facilities. Such an arrangement is technically conceivable, however.

3. The specific format for these figures has been taken from an unpublished report by Edward L. Warner III and David Ochmanek, "Future Options for the US-Soviet Strategic Arms Negotiations at Geneva: A US Perspective," revision of a paper presented at a conference on extended deterrence and arms control, March 1986 (Santa Monica, Calif.: Rand Corp., 1986).

FIGURE 1. **Assumptions for drawdown curves**

- All strategic warheads are on 100 percent alert and available to attack the other side.

- All weapons are essentially 100 percent reliable.

- The forces are unwarned and on day-to-day alert. C^3I is assumed effective so that alert forces are released for use.

- Silo-based ICBMs are at 100 percent alert and ready to fire.

- For the baseline case (figure 2) and the 6,000-warhead cases A, B, and C (figures 3, 5, and 7), all nuclear ballistic missile submarines (SSBNs) are on 50 percent alert. For the 3,000-warhead cases D, E, and F (figures 4, 6, and 8), all SSBNs are on 60 percent alert except U.S. Tridents, which are at 70 percent. Non-alert submarines are based at a few ports and are vulnerable. Alert submarines are assumed invulnerable.

- For the baseline and cases A, B, and C, bombers are on 30 percent alert. Non-alert bombers are at a relatively few airfields and are readily destroyed. U.S. alert bombers are subject to submarine-launched ballistic missile (SLBM) attack on the airfields and to barrage attacks during flyout. U.S. bombers based near the coast are most vulnerable. The segments marked "U.S. alert bombers" on figures 2, 3, 5, and 7 depict the drawdown under barrage of U.S. bombers as they are currently based and for typical assumptions about bomber takeoff time, flyout speed, hardness, and so on. Alert Soviet bombers are assumed to be based too far inland to permit effective barrage attacks. Their non-alert bombers (70 percent) are destroyed.

- For the 3,000-warhead cases D, E, and F, all bombers are assumed on 50 percent alert. U.S. as well as Soviet bombers are based inland so that barrage attack is impractical.

- All single-warhead land-mobile ICBMs are assumed sufficiently hardened or dispersed so as to require 5 attacking warheads to kill 1 missile and warhead. The day-to-day alert rate of mobile ICBMs is 75 percent for the baseline and cases A, B, and C, and 80 percent for cases D, E, and F.

- For the baseline and cases A, B, and C, ICBM silos are assumed to be attacked by 2 warheads per silo in most cases. In the baseline case and case A, a 3-on-1 attack is also shown for U.S. attacks on the USSR. All silos are assumed attacked by 3 warheads each for cases D and F. Case E has no silos.

- Both sides are assumed capable of launching under attack or on warning. Curves indicating such a launch are labeled "LUA" (figures 2 and 3).

Note: On all drawdown curves, dashed-line segments indicate barrage attacks on bombers and mobile ICBMs or, in the case of attacks on silo-based ICBMs, the possible unavailability of enough appropriate weapons to attack all silos.

15

It is assumed for both the United States and the Soviet Union that command authorities are always able to confer as required and to communicate to all weapon systems, including those on submarines, so that they can be targeted and released for use as needed. This is an important assumption and is obviously questionable, especially for retaliatory forces, in that many command system assets are highly vulnerable, and the system's integrity as a whole is difficult to assess.

The other assumptions tend to maximize the capabilities of the side striking first. For example, the forces on that side are assumed 100 percent alert and 100 percent reliable. Implicit in the statements about the vulnerability of forces of the side attacked is the assumption of high effectiveness for the attacker. Our assumptions about the side attacked, though not unreasonable, tend to understate alert status and thus survivability. Overall our assumptions are most appropriate to a classic "bolt-from-the-blue" first strike with the attacker at peak alert and capability and with the victim unwarned.

For our analyses the nuclear ballistic missile submarine (SSBN) forces at sea are *assumed invulnerable*. As a result, no hypothetical first strike can disarm the other side. From the U.S. standpoint, this is the most important assumption made.

A force element is termed "alert" if it is able to act immediately on receiving the command to do so (for example, launch missiles or aircraft). The assumption that the attacked side is on only day-to-day alert when the attacker makes its first strike is actually rather improbable, since it means that the victim has failed to act on any intelligence warning of strike preparations by the other side, or on any other political or military indications. The assumption does display the greatest advantage that a "first-striker" might be thought to have. Forces that would adequately survive attack under such alert conditions may be presumed to survive even better against more realistic challenges.

Most day-to-day alert rates in figure 1 were chosen based on published unclassified estimates for current forces.[4] For silo-

4. See, for example, CBO, *Modernizing*; and Cochran and others, *Nuclear Weapons Databook*.

based ICBMs the 100 percent rate is a reasonable approximation. For mobile ICBMs there is little experience. The choice of 75 percent seems like a good design goal if such missiles are to contribute significantly to total forces. The bomber alert rate of 30 percent is a standard assumption for U.S. aircraft. Currently the Soviet Union does not appear to maintain bombers on alert. They could presumably maintain a 30 percent level. The alert rate assumption of 50 percent for submarine forces (for the baseline and 6,000-warhead cases) is somewhat low for current U.S. forces and high for those of the Soviet Union. For future forces both sides could attain rates of at least 50 percent. The generally higher alert rates assumed for the 3,000-warhead cases are probably sustainable and affordable at these greatly reduced force levels. We presume that both sides would put a premium on high alert rates at these levels.

In figure 1 we state that each ICBM silo is attacked by either 2 or 3 warheads. On the drawdown curves we have approximated the consequences of either a 2-on-1 or a 3-on-1 attack by assuming *all* the silos are destroyed. Obviously this is an overestimate. A 2-on-1 attack that destroyed 99 percent of all silos would require an "effective" single-shot kill probability of 90 percent. (By "effective" probability we mean the overall probability of a single warhead destroying a silo, calculated on the basis of system reliability, weapon yield and accuracy, and silo hardness.) Admittedly, 90 percent is a high effective kill probability. On the other hand, a 2-on-1 attack that would destroy 90 percent of all silos requires only a 70 percent single-shot kill probability, and that value is not unreasonably high. In some cases we have shown 3-on-1 attacks for comparison or because we assumed that at lower force levels (for example, 3,000 warheads), very hard silos would be built requiring heavier attacks. For a 3-on-1 attack, a one-shot kill probability of 54 percent gives an overall destruction of 90 percent, again a credible value even against very hard targets. In the general spirit of our assumptions, which have assigned maximum capabilities to the offense, we think the estimates of silo destruction are reasonable.

FIGURE 2. **Drawdown curves: Baseline case—Current forces (10,000 warheads)**

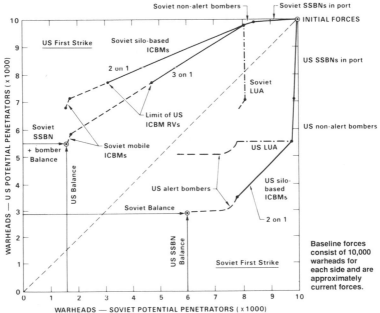

Figure 2 displays drawdown curves for current U.S. and Soviet forces. We will discuss this figure in some detail because it shows important aspects of the baseline case, and because the discussion applies qualitatively to the figures for the six reduced-force cases.

For the baseline case, both sides begin with 10,000 warheads, each a "potential penetrator" against the forces of the other side. The results of a Soviet first strike are shown to the right of the dashed diagonal line representing equal warheads for each side. The first drawdown segment, which begins at the "initial forces" point in the upper right corner, is for an attack on U.S. submarines in their ports. From table 1 the United States has a total of 5,760 submarine-launched ballistic missile (SLBM) warheads, of which 50 percent are assumed to be in port. We assume that 50 attacking Soviet warheads would destroy all non-alert submarines; SSBNs in port are very lucrative targets.

Non-alert U.S. heavy bombers at airbases are the next target.

The United States is assumed to have a total of 180 heavy bombers capable of carrying 2,160 warheads. Seventy percent of the bombers are not on alert and are assumed readily destroyed by 100 attacking Soviet warheads. Destruction of these 126 bombers eliminates the delivery capability for about 1,500 warheads. Whether the warheads themselves are actually destroyed is a secondary consideration.

The next segment is an attack on American ICBM silos. The United States has 1,000 silos containing 2,100 warheads. A Soviet attack with 2 warheads against each silo is assumed to destroy essentially all U.S. ICBM warheads. At this point on the drawdown curve, 2,150 Soviet warheads have destroyed almost 6,500 U.S. warheads.

An alternate ICBM drawdown path is shown, labeled "US LUA." The assumption for this path is that the United States, sensing a massive launch of Soviet missiles, launches its own ICBMs before most Soviet warheads arrive. It is also possible, in principle, to launch under attack at least some missiles from submarines in port, but we have not included that path on the drawdown curves. There are well-recognized dangers to relying on launch under attack (LUA) for deterrence, but the side contemplating a first strike must face the possibility that it would suffer a full ICBM retaliatory strike if the struck side is technically capable of such a launch.

The final segment of the curve is for U.S. alert bombers. Fifty-four bombers (30 percent) carrying 648 warheads are on high alert. To destroy any of these bombers the Soviets must hit them during the relatively short time before they take off and disperse following warning. The usual attack scenario envisages Soviet submarines launching their missiles from positions close to American shores. Alert bombers on U.S. airbases near the coasts might be destroyed even before takeoff. Those based well inland could be destroyed only by a barrage of the area surrounding the airbase; the farther inland, the larger the required barrage area. The drawdown segment for alert bombers is shown curved to indicate schematically the mixture of SAC airbases near the coasts and inland. We estimate that as many as 1,800 Soviet SLBM warheads would be needed to barrage-attack all fifty-four U.S. alert heavy bombers successfully, with most attacks directed against the inland airbases. Because 1,800 warheads is almost 60 percent of the Soviet SLBM force, we conclude such an inefficient use of forces is unlikely, and thus show this barrage attack as a dashed curve to suggest that it and similar attacks might be considered impractical.

At the endpoint of the drawdown curve for a Soviet first strike against the United States, assuming the alert bombers were barraged, the Soviets would still have about 6,000 warheads. The United States would have almost 3,000 warheads on about eighteen submarines at sea. Our assumption that these submarines are invulnerable is obviously critical. If the United States had exercised the LUA option, an additional 2,100 ICBM warheads would have been launched against the Soviet Union.

The results of a U.S. first strike against the strategic forces of the Soviet Union are displayed to the left of the diagonal in figure 2. Because the Soviet force mix (see table 2) is different from that of the United States, the drawdown curve looks somewhat different. The first segment is again for submarines in port, here with a capacity to carry 1,536 warheads, all of which are assumed destroyed by about 50 attacking U.S. warheads. The next element in the curve, the Soviet heavy bomber force, is assumed capable of carrying 500 warheads and to have 30 percent of the aircraft on alert. We assume it is impractical for the United States to destroy the 54 Soviet alert bombers because the bases are too far inland. Thus the 150 warheads on alert bombers could be used in retaliation against the United States. The 126 heavy bombers not on alert (70 percent), capable of carrying 350 warheads, are assumed destroyed on their airbases by 100 U.S. warheads.

Most Soviet strategic warheads are on ICBMs based in hard silos. We estimate (table 2) there are 6,348 warheads on 1,326 missiles in silos. Attacking every silo with 2 U.S. ICBM warheads, currently the only appropriate U.S. weapon for a prompt attack, would require more than the total U.S. inventory of about 2,100 ICBM warheads. We show drawdown segments for all the ICBM warheads for both 2-on-1 and 3-on-1 attacks but indicate the points on the segments where the United States would exhaust its inventory of U.S. ICBM warheads. Because of the presumed hardness of Soviet silos, a 3-on-1 ratio would be needed for a very effective attack.

A slightly more accurate treatment of the Soviet ICBM drawdown would take account of the fact that half of all Soviet missiles (that is, the SS-18s and SS-19s) account for 80 percent of Soviet ICBM warheads. A 3-on-1 attack of just these silos would require 2,000 U.S. ICBM warheads.

The Soviets are deploying the SS-25, a mobile single-warhead ICBM. There were some 70 SS-25s in early 1986. Alert mobile ICBMs would be deployed so that a barrage of several attacking U.S. warheads would be needed to destroy each one. In this and all other cases, we have assumed that 5 attacking warheads are needed to kill one U.S. or Soviet mobile missile. (This figure is consistent with the nominal design goal for the U.S. small ICBM, or SICBM.)[5] Assuming that 75 percent of the 70 SS-25s are on alert, it would require about 260 attacking warheads in barrage to destroy them.

To sum up the U.S. first strike: assuming a 3-on-1 attack on all silos, about 4,400 U.S. warheads are used and 5,600 remain. The attack would destroy, by this overstated estimate, about 8,300 Soviet warheads and leave 150 bomber weapons and 1,536 SLBM warheads for Soviet retaliation. If only SS-18 and SS-19 silos were destroyed, another 1,100 silo-based Soviet ICBM warheads would survive. If the Soviets exercised a launch-under-attack option, as many as 6,300 Soviet ICBM warheads could survive to be used in immediate retaliation, and the Soviets would still have the 1,700 SLBM and bomber weapons for other uses.

Based on these admittedly simplified characterizations of U.S. and Soviet first strikes with current forces, with assumptions that result in substantial overestimates of the attacker's advan-

5. Peter Clausen, Allan Krass, and Robert Zirkle, *In Search of Stability: An Assessment of New U.S. Nuclear Forces* (Cambridge, Mass.: Union of Concerned Scientists, 1986), p. 17.

tage, it appears that either side as the aggressor would have to face retaliation by at least roughly 3,000 surviving warheads. The added possibility of a launch under attack by ICBMs greatly increases the retaliation threat. So far as these results apply, neither side has a rational incentive for a surprise first strike. In a crisis so severe that nuclear attack seemed possible, both sides would be at highest alert. Should either side consider preemption, it would have to face the likelihood of even greater retaliation than in the case of surprise attack.

Figures 3 through 8 are drawdown curves for the six reduced-force cases, A through F. The curves are constructed on essentially the same basis as the baseline case curves (figure 2). Note that the scales are different from figure to figure. For the 3,000-warhead cases, we have assumed that both sides would take added measures for improved survivability, including higher alert rates, increased silo hardening, and more inland basing of bombers (by the United States) to make barrage attacks impractical.

In case A, at 6,000 warheads, both sides' forces are reduced more or less proportionally from the baseline forces. The only modernization is the replacement of the U.S. B-52 by the B-1 bomber. The present asymmetries in force mixtures are perpetuated. Figure 3 shows drawdown curves for case A. Comparison with figure 2 shows essentially the same drawdown patterns but with reduced numbers. Recalling again that the assumptions exaggerate the effectiveness of first strikes, one can see that each side, following an attack, could expect to have 1,500 to 2,000 surviving warheads for retaliation. Launching under attack would, again, substantially increase the strength of the retaliation.

Case D at 3,000 warheads (figure 4) is a further proportional reduction from case A. No new systems are incorporated, but there is some increase in emphasis on the more survivable systems, and the Soviets can no longer barrage U.S. bombers. Because we assume the Soviet Union will continue to emphasize fixed MIRVed ICBMs, Soviet forces for retaliation after a U.S. first strike are about 1,000 warheads and the impetus to launch

FIGURE 3. **Drawdown curves: Case A—Proportionally reduced forces (6,000 warheads)**

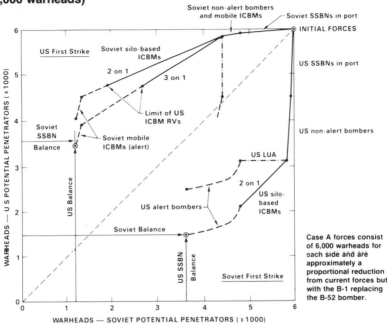

FIGURE 4. **Drawdown curves: Case D—Proportionally reduced forces (3,000 warheads)**

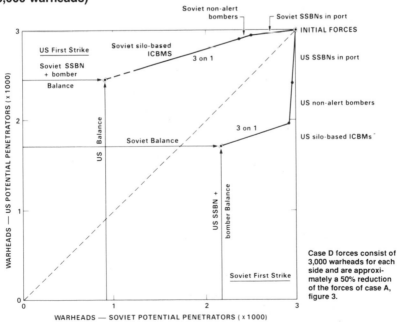

under attack is greater. After a Soviet attack the surviving U.S. forces of about 1,700 warheads are comparable with the unused Soviet forces.

In case B, at 6,000 warheads, both sides are assumed to increase emphasis on highly survivable forces. All 1,000 U.S. ICBMs are single-warhead mobile missiles. The Soviet Union, still emphasizing ICBMs, makes half of its 2,000 ICBMs mobile SS-25s. Both sides place almost half their forces on submarines. Figure 5 shows the drawdown curves. If either side attempts to barrage-attack the mobile missiles, assumed to require 5 attacking warheads per missile destroyed, the final forces after the attacks are essentially equal, or there is a disadvantage to the attacker. If the barrage is not attempted, the attacker has a large relative advantage but must face retaliation by more than 2,500 warheads.

The forces of case E at 3,000 warheads are essentially symmetrical, with both sides assumed to have 1,000 mobile single-warhead missiles and about 1,500 SLBM warheads. The drawdown curves for case E in figure 6 show that neither side has enough warheads to barrage all the mobile missiles. If they cannot strike the mobile missiles or the submarines, both sides would have to face more than 2,000 warheads in retaliation after a first strike.

Case C at 6,000 warheads emphasizes both increased survivability and offensive capability. The United States, in particular, chooses a force mix of 500 MX warheads on 50 missiles and 500 mobile ICBMs, and deploys the accurate and relatively high-yield Trident D-5 missile warhead. The Soviets deploy 2,000 ICBM warheads, half of them on mobile missiles, 2,800 modern SLBM warheads, and 1,200 weapons on the new Blackjack bomber. Figure 7 displays the drawdown curves. The outcome of first strikes is not greatly influenced by the assumed offensive capabilities of either side. The drawdown results are similar to the results in figure 5 for a more survivable force mixture of an equal number of warheads. A Soviet first strike that included a successful barrage of U.S. alert bombers and mobile missiles would leave a retaliatory force of more than 1,400 U.S. warheads.

FIGURE 5. **Drawdown curves: Case B—Maximum mobility forces (6,000 warheads)**

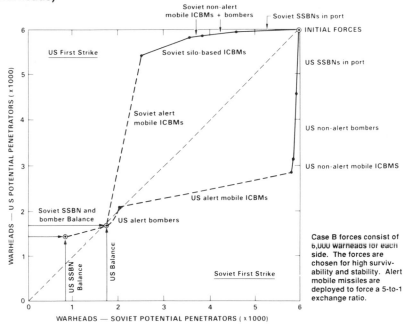

Case B forces consist of 6,000 warheads for each side. The forces are chosen for high survivability and stability. Alert mobile missiles are deployed to force a 5-to-1 exchange ratio.

FIGURE 6. **Drawdown curves: Case E—Maximum mobility forces (3,000 warheads)**

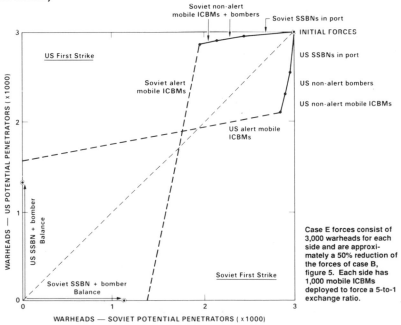

Case E forces consist of 3,000 warheads for each side and are approximately a 50% reduction of the forces of case B, figure 5. Each side has 1,000 mobile ICBMs deployed to force a 5-to-1 exchange ratio.

FIGURE 7. **Drawdown curves: Case C—Modernized forces (6,000 warheads)**

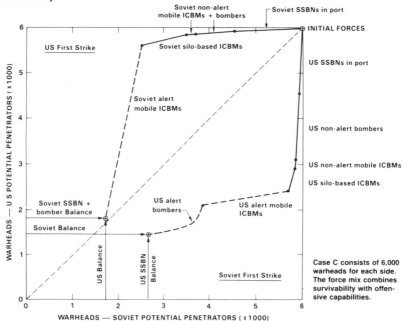

FIGURE 8. **Drawdown curves: Case F—Modernized forces (3,000 warheads)**

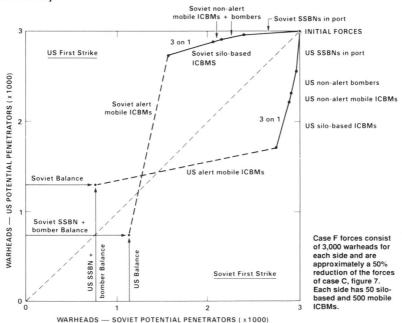

26

A U.S. first strike that included a barrage of all Soviet mobile missiles would leave a retaliatory force of more than 1,800 Soviet warheads. If either side passed up the barrage option in the first strike, it would face retaliatory forces of more than 2,500 warheads.

Figure 8 displays the drawdown results for case F with 3,000 warheads. Like case C, these forces combine offensive capability with survivability. The forces are almost identical in makeup, the slight asymmetry in drawdown curves attributable to the higher alert rate assumed for the U.S. Trident submarines. After a first strike by either side that included a barrage of mobile missiles, the attacker would have fewer than 800 remaining warheads and face retaliation by more than 1,200 warheads. Without the barrage the attacker would face retaliation by more than 1,500 warheads.

How many of its warheads are expected to survive is one important measure of the deterrent capability of the attacked force. In addition, the ratio of surviving attacker-to-attacked warheads is of some importance. The lower the ratio, the less "advantage" there is, even in the narrowest terms, to the attack. Table 3 summarizes the outcome for the United States and the Soviet Union of the cases illustrated in figures 2–8, taken at the final point on the drawdown curves. The final segments of the curves (shown dashed) represent the most difficult tasks for the attacker—those requiring the most resources per warhead destroyed. If the attacker chose not to strike these forces, it would have a better relative position (that is, a higher attacker-to-attacked warhead ratio) but at the cost of facing a larger absolute number of surviving enemy warheads. Presenting an attacker with such "no-win" choices is a major function of such vulnerable-at-a-price force elements as alert bombers and mobile missiles.

In cases B, C, E, and F, 50 percent or more of the ICBM warheads are on single-warhead mobile missiles. For the drawdown analyses, *alert* mobile missiles of both sides are assumed to require a barrage attack with 5 attacking warheads per mobile warhead destroyed. Though the survivability of such a mobile

TABLE 3. **Attacker-to-survivor ratios after drawdown**

Item	Baseline	A	B	C	D	E	F
				Case			
			SOVIET FIRST STRIKE				
1. Remaining Soviet warheads	6,000	3,600	800	2,600	2,200	0[a]	700
2. Surviving U.S. SLBM and bomber warheads	2,900	1,500	1,400	1,400	1,400	1,300[b]	1,300
3. Ratio of row 1 to row 2	2.1	2.4	0.6	1.9	1.6	0.0	0.5
			U.S. FIRST STRIKE				
4. Remaining U.S. warheads	5,600	3,600	1,700	1,800	2,500	0[a]	700
5. Surviving Soviet SLBM and bomber warheads	1,700	1,300	1,700	1,800	900	1,400[b]	1,200
6. Ratio of row 4 to row 5	3.3	2.8	1.0	1.0	2.8	0.0	0.6

a. Zero attacker warheads remain in case E because the attacker is assumed to exhaust all its forces in barrage attacks of the other side's mobile ICBMs. In fact, such exhaustion attacks would almost surely not occur.

b. Surviving warheads for this case include mobile ICBM warheads that cannot be attacked because attacking warheads are exhausted.

system is very good, the costs and operational difficulties are likely to be high, at least for the United States. Basing new single-warhead missiles in fixed silos is a less survivable but potentially less costly alternative to mobile basing, and it has received some consideration.[6] U.S. emphasis has been on superhard silos, but some planners have suggested basing in old Minuteman silos or similar new silos also.[7]

Superhard silos would require an attacker to expend at least 3 warheads for high confidence of success, while Minuteman and similar silos would each require at least 2 attacking warheads. In addition, silo-based missiles could be near 100 percent alert at all times, which is unlikely to be the case for mobile basing. Qualitatively, drawdown results that assume silo basing of single-warhead missiles would be similar to those for mobile basing.

6. Brent Scowcroft, chairman, and others, *Report of the President's Commission on Strategic Forces (Scowcroft Commission Report)* (Washington, D.C.: Department of Defense, 1983).

7. Richard L. Garwin, "A Blueprint for Radical Weapons Cuts," *Bulletin of the Atomic Scientists*, vol. 44 (March 1988), pp. 10–13.

Clearly the results of the drawdown analyses are determined by the various assumptions discussed earlier. Of all the conditions determining how many warheads will survive attack, the most important is our assumption that alert submarines at sea are invulnerable. It is also a defensible assumption for the present. None of the cases investigated suggests that a disarming surprise first strike is now or soon will be feasible for either side.

As for stability of the forces under conditions of severe crisis, there are some obvious differences among the several force models. The drawdown curves of forces chosen for maximum survivability, cases B (6,000 warheads) and E (3,000 warheads), suggest that the attacker would be worse off than his victim (in the narrow sense of remaining warheads) after a preemptive attack. For the modernized forces, cases C and F, the enhancement of offensive capability (hard target kill capability), as well as increased survivability, assumed comparable for both sides, does not greatly change the apparent stability seen for cases B and E. The proportionally reduced forces, cases A and D, are less satisfactory for stability during severe crisis; they perpetuate current asymmetries and fail to include significant new elements with enhanced survivability.

Drawdown curves like those discussed in this section are useful graphic devices to display the elements of vulnerability (or lack thereof) to surprise attack of opposing strategic nuclear forces. They do not, however, show what would happen to military targets besides strategic nuclear forces in a full exchange of forces, first strike and retaliation. Simulations of such exchanges for the various opposing force structures are discussed in the next section.

FOUR

Exchange Calculations

*I*n this section we use computer simulations of nuclear exchanges to look at how well each force model would accomplish a set of military tasks, both in a first strike and in retaliation. The tasks are quantified as specified amounts of damage to the targets that make up the bulk of each side's ability to wage the war, such as ICBM silos, strategic airfields, and key military industries.[8] We consider the effects of the various nuclear exchanges on a Soviet target set that we believe to be consistent with U.S. strategic targeting policy as it has been presented and discussed publicly.[9] We do the same evaluations for the Soviet side, based on assumptions about Soviet targeting policy. Though little definite is known to us about Soviet targeting, reasonable hypotheses can be made, and such evaluations may cast light on what the effects would be for different target sets.

We used a computer model, the "Arsenal Exchange Model" (AEM), which has been employed in the defense community

8. See, for example, Desmond Ball and Jeffrey Richelson, eds., *Strategic Nuclear Targeting* (Ithaca: Cornell University Press, 1986).

9. *Scowcroft Commission Report; Department of Defense Annual Report to the Congress, Fiscal Year 1982* (GPO, 1981), pp. 38–45; and Leon Sloss and Marc Dean Millot, "U.S. Nuclear Strategy in Evolution," *Strategic Review*, vol. 12 (Winter 1984), pp. 19–28.

for twenty years.[10] AEM takes as input weapon and target data, instructions specifying desired coverage and damage for each target type supplied, and reserve requirements. The calculation program then makes the best choices it can from the weapons available to meet the attack objectives.

We used available statements, mainly from Department of Defense sources, to develop lists of U.S. and Soviet target types of military importance consistent with stated U.S. targeting policies and with what is understood of Soviet policies.[11] The lists include ICBM silos, strategic submarine bases and bomber airfields, and in a highly aggregated manner, installations such as air, naval, and army bases, military headquarters, government centers, and military industries. Some other industrial plants, such as power stations and petroleum refineries, are included because of their military importance.

Table 4 shows the targets for the baseline case. Six general target categories are defined and, within each category, the subcategories of target types we used in the exchange calculations. (For the calculations, operational silos are actually broken down into the specific missile types.) The table also

10. For a description of the Arsenal Exchange Model see William L. Cotsworth, *The Arsenal Exchange Model (AEM): Management Summary*, Rpt. S-83-009-DEN (Englewood, Colo.: Stonehouse Group, 1983). The AEM uses several sophisticated mathematical processes to support the required calculations. For damage calculations, statistical methods are used to calculate probabilities of damage to targets by various types of weapons. These calculations follow standard damage methodology as widely practiced in the strategic analysis community. For the allocation process the model uses variations of standard linear programming techniques and decomposition techniques to allocate weapons to targets. The mathematical algorithms used by the AEM are designed to produce optimal allocation. Recently a computer model, apparently similar to AEM, has been developed in the Soviet Union and used there for assessments of force reductions. Few details are available on either the computer program or the calculational results. A recent report on the Soviet work contains conclusions, some of which are similar to those of our study. Roald Sagdeyev and Andrei Kokoshin, eds., *Strategic Stability under Conditions of Radical Nuclear Arms Reductions*, report on a Study of the Committee of Soviet Scientists for Peace against the Nuclear Threat, 2d ed. (Moscow, November 1987).

11. *Department of Defense Annual Report to the Congress, Fiscal Year 1981*, and later years; Department of Defense, *Soviet Military Power 1986* and earlier editions; Desmond Ball, *Targeting for Strategic Deterrence*, Adelphi Paper 185 (London: International Institute for Strategic Studies, 1983); and William W. Kaufmann, *A Reasonable Defense* (Brookings, 1986), table 5-9, p. 82, and personal communication.

TABLE 4. **Baseline case targets**

General category	Number of targets[a]		Target types (subcategories)
	U.S.	USSR	
ICBM silos and launch control facilities	1,110	1,460	Launch control facilities Operational silos Training silos
Bomber, SSBN, and mobile ICBM bases	130	330	SSBN bases (ports) Bomber airbases—primary Bomber airbases—dispersal or alternate Mobile ICBM bases IRBM and MRBM bases
Other military forces	1,080	1,560	Airbases Naval ports and bases Ground forces Nuclear weapon facilities and storage Antiballistic missile sites Early warning radars Air defense sites Logistic support centers Conventional ammunition storage
Government and C³I facilities and centers	720	1,080	Civil government Military headquarters Military command posts Military communications Other communications
Military manufacturing	1,040	1,000	Major weapon end-product manufacturing Other military manufacturing—large Other military manufacturing—medium
Refineries and electric power	1,920	520	Refineries Electric power stations Petroleum stores

Sources: Target numbers are derived from sources in text note 11 and the authors' estimates.

a. Targets are in the United States and Soviet Union only. All target numbers are for the baseline case. Total numbers change for reduced-force cases only for the first two categories.

gives the number of individual targets in each nation by category. For the baseline case, we estimated that the total number of *significant targets* for each side is about the same, roughly 6,000, although the distribution among types differs.

Besides characterizing the targets by number, we supplied data on their estimated vulnerability. Most targets on our lists, other than silos, are relatively "soft" and do not require high-yield accurate weapons to damage them. Although population centers in themselves have not been targeted, the damage to people and to civilian installations would, of course, be very great, and we consider it in our next section, Civil Damage.

In the calculation program, available weapons are allocated to targets according to their military potential or value. Lucrative targets like naval bases with strategic submarines in port, and airbases with non-alert bombers, have precedence over ICBM silos with fewer weapons per target. *The program considers all targets of a type (subcategory) identical and at fixed locations.* All SS-18 silos, for example, are assumed identical and have equal priority. But different types of ICBMs have been assigned different relative priorities. Thus SS-11 silos with their single-warhead missiles have less value and thus lower priority than SS-18 silos with 10 warheads each. Primary strategic airbases have higher value and priority than secondary or dispersal bases, and large critical military industries have higher priority than medium military industry targets. Table 4 shows the target types in approximate order of their assumed military priority within each category.

The fact that a number of potential targets is specified on our lists does not mean that all the targets must be attacked. Desired levels of target coverage and damage are specified for each target type. For example, one might target for severe damage and 90 percent coverage of all ICBM silos, SSBN bases, and strategic airfields, while accepting 30 percent to 40 percent coverage of military industry targets and perhaps 20 percent to 30 percent coverage for electric power stations. Note, however, that because of the different military values of the target types in our six general categories, a given number of targets destroyed will generally represent an even larger fraction of the total military value destroyed.

The choice of targets of greatest military importance and the degree to which they should be attacked represent the authors' informed judgments and common sense. Within reasonable limits, simulation results are not very sensitive to these judgments. We have assumed that mobile ICBMs and alert bombers, as well as SSBNs at sea, cannot usefully be and are not attacked by barrage or other means. Bomber bases are attacked, as are

TABLE 5. **Weapon system characteristics**[a]

System	Yield (kilotons)	Accuracy (circular error probable, in meters)
U.S. systems		
Minuteman 2	1,200	630
Minuteman 3	170	220
Minuteman 3A	335	220
MX	335	90
SICBM	475	130
Poseidon C-3	40	460
Poseidon/Trident C-4	100	460
Trident D-5	475	130
Air-launched cruise missile	200	90
Soviet systems		
SS-11	950	1,400
SS-13	600	1,850
SS-17	750	320
SS-18	500	250[b]
SS-19	550	300[b]
SS-25	500	190
SS-N-6	750	930
SS-N-8	750	930
SS-N-17	1,000[b]	1,400[b]
SS-N-18	500	560
SS-N-20	100	560
SS-N-23	100[c]	560[c]
Air-launched cruise missile	200[d]	90[d]

a. Unless otherwise noted, all yields and CEPs are from U.S. Congress, Congressional Budget Office, *Modernizing U.S. Strategic Offensive Forces: The Administration's Program and Alternatives* (Washington, D.C.: GPO, 1983), pp. 84, 86, 90.
b. Data from International Institute for Strategic Studies, *The Military Balance 1985–1986* (London, 1985), pp. 162–63.
c. Assumed identical to values for SS-N-20.
d. Assumed identical to values for U.S. ALCM.

mobile ICBM base areas, but the alert aircraft and missiles are assumed to escape. Although they are important to military capability, mobile command, control, and communication (C^3) facilities and ground forces out of garrison are not included in our target set.

Target coverage and damage level achieved are conditioned also by the number of weapons available and their yields and accuracies. In our calculations the number of weapons attacking one ICBM silo is at most three. Table 5 shows the weapon yields and accuracies we used in the exchange calculations.

Other quantitative assumptions that were made for the simulations are summarized in figure 9. Because the AEM can

FIGURE 9. **Alert rate and reliability assumptions for exchange simulations**

FOR THE SIDE STRIKING FIRST (ALL CASES)

- First-strike forces are at generated alert.

- Alert rates for U.S. and Soviet forces are:
    1.0 for silo-based and mobile ICBMs
    0.7–0.75 for SLBMs
    0.95 for bombers.

- System reliabilities are 0.8 for missiles and 0.72 for bombers.

FOR THE SIDE RETALIATING AFTER RIDING OUT AN ATTACK OR WITH LUA

- Retaliating forces are on day-to-day alert.

For the baseline and 6,000-warhead cases A, B, and C

- Alert rates for U.S. forces are:
    0.85 for silo-based ICBMs
    0.75 for mobile ICBMs
    0.55–0.66 for SLBMs
    0.33 for bombers.

- Alert rates for Soviet forces are:
    0.85 for silo-based ICBMs
    0.75 for mobile ICBMs
    0.3 for SLBMs
    0.15 for bombers.

For the 3,000-warhead cases D, E, and F

- Alert rates for U.S. and Soviet forces are:
    0.95 for silo-based ICBMs
    0.8 for mobile ICBMs
    0.6 for SLBMs (except U.S. Tridents with 0.7)
    0.5 for bombers.

- System reliability for all retaliatory forces is 0.8 for missiles and 0.72 for bombers.

---

handle detailed inputs, the alert rate and reliability assumptions made for the exchange simulations differ somewhat from those for the drawdown curves, in a direction that we believe improves the realism of the simulation. As with the drawdown scenarios, however, the worst-case assumption is made that first-strike forces are always at generated or maximum alert, while attacked forces are on day-to-day alert.

We introduce system reliability factors for both first-strike and retaliatory forces. System reliability is defined as the probability of successful launch and transit to the target area, assuming that the launch order has been successfully communicated. It does not include the estimate of the probability of hitting and damaging the target, which depends on CEP (circular error probable, a measure of accuracy), yield, and target hardness. This "end game" calculation is done separately for each target and attacking weapon. We do not know actual system reliabilities, but we thought it worthwhile to use some rough guesses rather than stay with the assumption of 100 percent reliability used for the drawdown analyses, where reliability does not affect the results significantly. We have assumed plausible values of 0.8 for all ICBMs and SLBMs and 0.72 for bomber weapons, primarily cruise missiles. The value for bombers is derived by assuming 80 percent reliability with an assumed 90 percent penetration probability to give the Soviet Union some minimal credit for defense against the cruise missiles.

For each attack scenario, a strategic reserve is specified, usually 10 percent of the total force. The reserve is specified for retaliatory attacks as well as first strikes unless the available forces are too small to meet minimal coverage needs. Strategic reserve requirements established by the United States and the Soviet Union are unknown to us, but it would be difficult for either defense establishment to overlook the possibility that weapons will be needed after the initial exchanges. Reference to the figures (discussed below) displaying the results of the exchange simulations and to table 6 permits one to compare the 10 percent reserve forces desired with the actual number of surviving weapon systems estimated in the calculations.

It is again assumed, as it was for the drawdown analyses, that command authorities on both sides can confer and can communicate to all weapon systems, including those on submarines, at all times, and that those systems can be targeted as required.[12] For the side striking first, it is probably an

12. Ashton B. Carter, "Assessing Command System Vulnerability," in Carter, John

acceptable assumption. For the side attacked, perfect command and intelligence survival is unlikely, but it is very difficult to estimate the probable damage to C³I and the consequences for retaliation. It is the task of those responsible for C³I on both sides to design and operate command systems that are sufficiently survivable, through hardening and mobility, and redundant enough to ensure the capability for retaliation with limited degradation. For deterrence, a potential attacker should always have to assume that the other side's command system would function well enough after attack to permit all surviving weapons to be released, targeted, and delivered. To analyze departures from the assumption of perfect C³I would require a separate study. In this as in other areas, this analysis can only urge that C³I survival be considered in the context of arms reduction.

The nuclear force structures we evaluated were the same baseline and six reduced-force cases described earlier. For each case, six simulation calculations were done: a Soviet first strike, a Soviet retaliatory strike with ICBM launch under attack (LUA), a Soviet retaliatory strike after receiving, or "riding out," a U.S. first strike, and the three analogous U.S. attacks.

Though the United States and the Soviet Union have stated that they will not start a war by initiating a strategic first strike, both sides presumably consider what would happen if the other side were to strike first. In a negotiating context, it is useful to understand how first strikes are viewed on both sides. Our assumptions are not sufficiently well informed to permit a good evaluation of the Soviet assessment, but they may give some idea of how a U.S. first strike would look to them. Much more work needs to be done to assess the existence and consequences of any asymmetry in target structure, weapon system characteristics, and perceptions between the two sides.

The histograms of figures 10 through 23 (discussed below) summarize the results of the various attack simulations. Each figure shows the simulation results for a first strike and for a retaliatory attack with rideout for one of the force cases and

D. Steinbruner, and Charles A. Zraket, eds., *Managing Nuclear Operations* (Brookings, 1987), pp. 555–610.

one of the countries. Results for Soviet attacks are shown first, followed by results for U.S. attacks.

Figures 24 and 25 illustrate the effects of launch under attack for the scenario in which it is most significant, case D. For the other cases, the target coverage results with LUA are essentially identical to first-strike results, if warning and communication are assumed to work in a timely way, and only the sizes of the reserve and residual forces vary from a first strike. We do not suggest that launch under attack is or ought to be a retaliatory posture for either country, but it is a technical possibility, and its contribution to deterring must be evaluated in the context of reduction negotiations.

For all the figures, 10 through 25, the left-hand histogram shows target coverage. The height of each histogram is the total number of targets in each of the general categories discussed earlier and listed in table 4. For each general-category bar, an upper line shows the number of the targets attacked, and a lower line and shading show the number destroyed. The number of targets destroyed is a convenient measure of the results of an attack, but as mentioned earlier, the numerical fraction of targets destroyed is always less than the fraction of military potential or value destroyed. For comparing target coverage between first strike and retaliation, or from case to case, however, the number of targets destroyed is a practical measure.

On the right side of each figure a second histogram summarizes the disposition of the forces—ICBMs, SLBMs, and bombers—involved in the simulation illustrated. Some abbreviations were necessary. The shaded areas marked "used" represent the number of warheads actually expended in the attack. The abbreviation "N-A" refers to forces that were not available because they were not on alert or were destroyed in a first strike by the other side. "S.R." means strategic reserve, assumed to be 10 percent of the initial warhead number, and "Resid." refers to residual forces available but not required for attack or for the strategic reserve.

We show the first strike and retaliatory strike carried out by each country on one page, rather than an "exchange" sequence with a first strike by one side displayed with the retaliatory strike by the other. Both displays are informative, but the former makes comparisons easier.

Figure 10 for the baseline case with 10,000 warheads illustrates the results of a Soviet first strike and a Soviet retaliation attack with rideout. For the first strike, all our assumed target coverage requirements are met, a 10 percent strategic reserve is maintained, and there are substantial residual Soviet forces. For the retaliation with rideout case, coverage of ICBM targets is limited, but all other targets are covered as well as in the first strike. The strategic reserve is still about 10 percent, but there are no residual forces.

Figure 11 is for the analogous U.S. attacks for the baseline case. Again, targets are satisfactorily covered, a reserve is maintained, and there are residual forces after a first strike. But note that, even in a first strike, U.S. coverage of ICBM targets is limited. This result follows from the assumed hardness of Soviet silos, the accuracies and yields of U.S. warheads, and our restriction that no more than 3 warheads be used against one silo. All other targets are covered as required both in first strike and retaliation.

The baseline target coverages displayed in figures 10 and 11 for Soviet and U.S. first strikes respectively represent our assumed target coverage objectives for each side in all simulation cases, with due allowance for changing numbers of missile targets from case to case.

Figures 12 and 13 are for case A, the 6,000-warhead proportional reduction case. The comments above on the baseline case apply almost without change to this case. Except for the ICBM silos, the number and coverage of all targets are essentially the same as in the baseline case. Residual forces in both first strikes are smaller than before but still ample. The desired strategic reserve is still 10 percent, or 600 warheads, and it is attained in all attacks except the Soviet retaliation, where it is only 100 warheads.

Figures 14 and 15 illustrate the results for case B, 6,000 warheads with high mobility. All U.S. ICBMs are mobile, while

FIGURE 10. **Exchange simulations: Baseline case—Current forces (10,000 warheads), Soviet attacks**

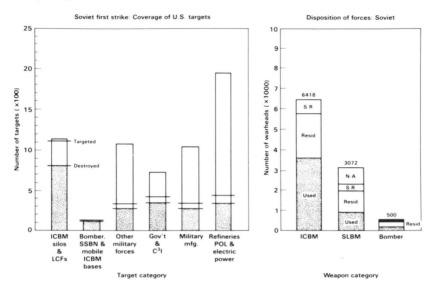

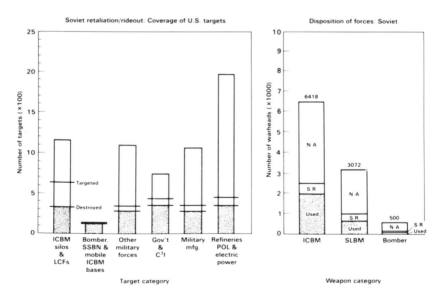

FIGURE 11. **Exchange simulations: Baseline case—Current forces (10,000 warheads), U.S. attacks**

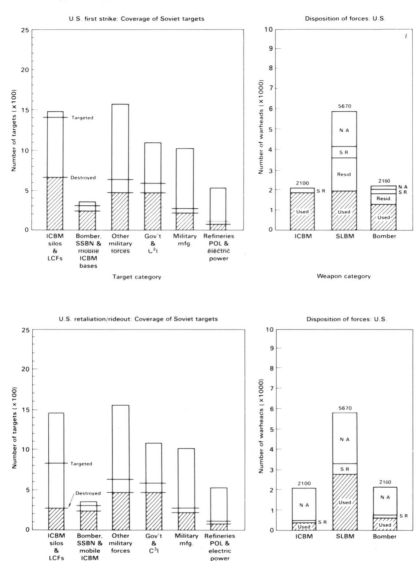

FIGURE 12. **Exchange simulations: Case A—Proportionally reduced forces (6,000 warheads), Soviet attacks**

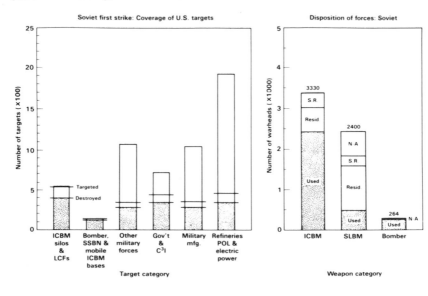

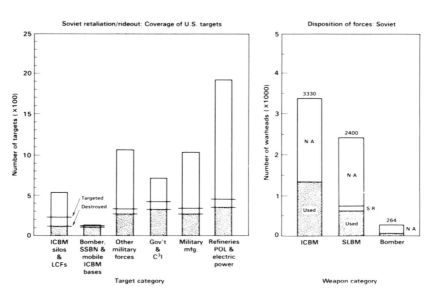

FIGURE 13. **Exchange simulations: Case A—Proportionally reduced forces (6,000 warheads), U.S. attacks**

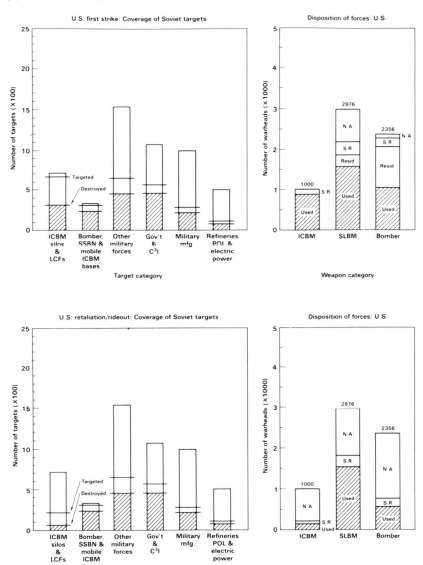

FIGURE 14. Exchange simulations: Case B—Maximum mobility forces (6,000 warheads), Soviet attacks

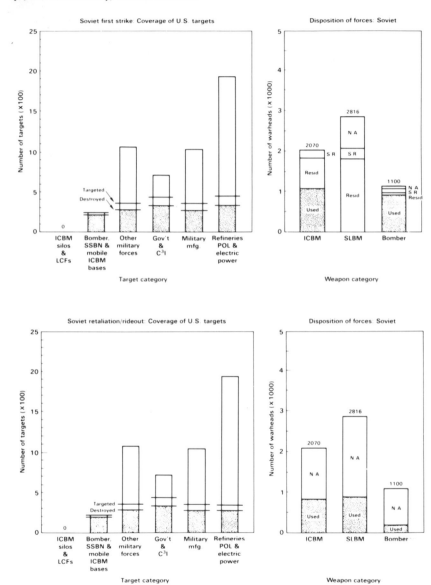

FIGURE 15. **Exchange simulations: Case B—Maximum mobility forces (6,000 warheads), U.S. attacks**

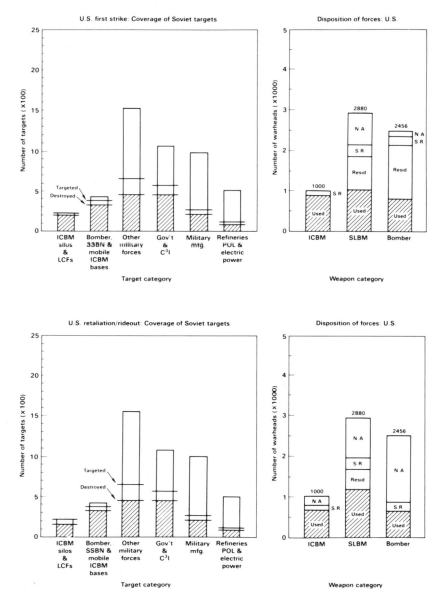

FIGURE 16. **Exchange simulations: Case C—Modernized forces (6,000 warheads), Soviet attacks**

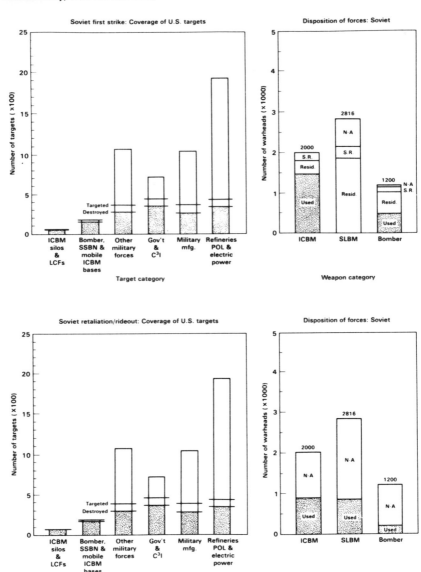

FIGURE 17. **Exchange simulations: Case C—Modernized forces (6,000 warheads), U.S. attacks**

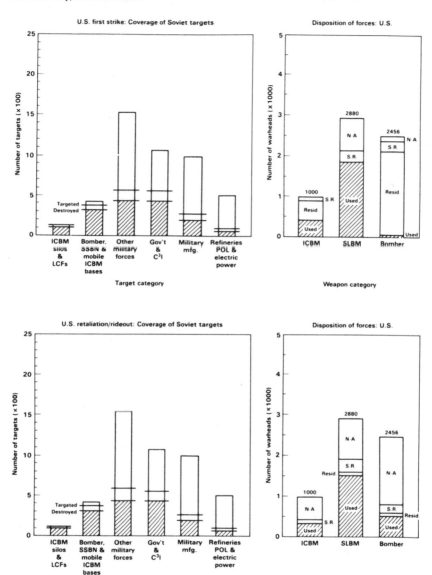

FIGURE 18. **Exchange simulations: Case D—Proportionally reduced forces (3,000 warheads), Soviet attacks**

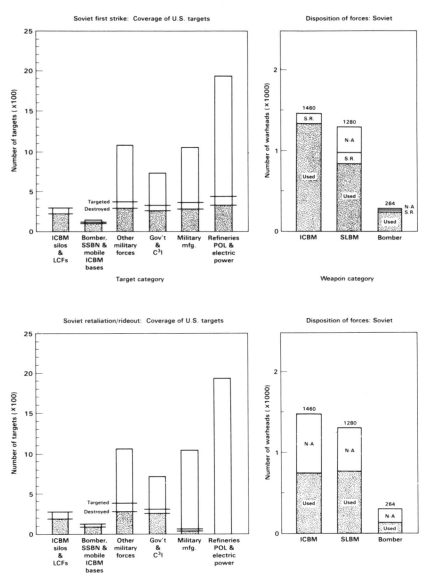

FIGURE 19. **Exchange simulations: Case D—Proportionally reduced forces (3,000 warheads), U.S. attacks**

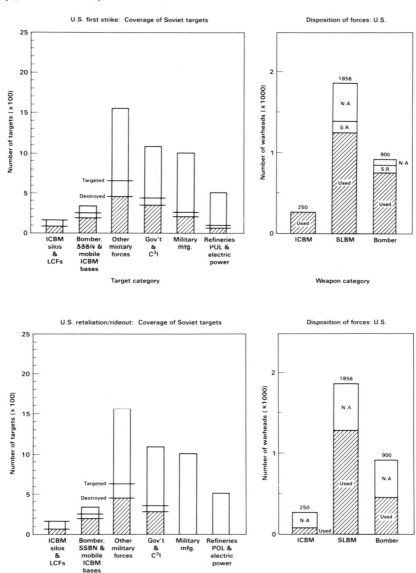

FIGURE 20. Exchange simulations: Case E—Maximum mobility forces (3,000 warheads), Soviet attacks

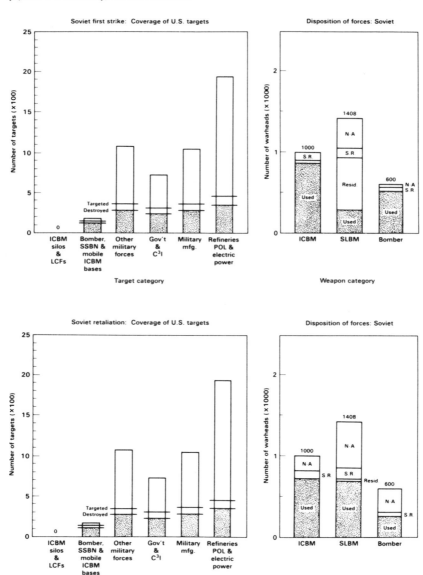

FIGURE 21. **Exchange simulations: Case E—Maximum mobility forces (3,000 warheads), U.S. attacks**

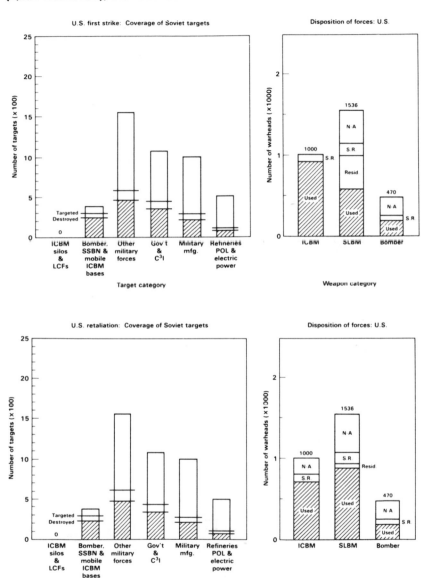

FIGURE 22. **Exchange simulations: Case F—Modernized forces (3,000 warheads), Soviet attacks**

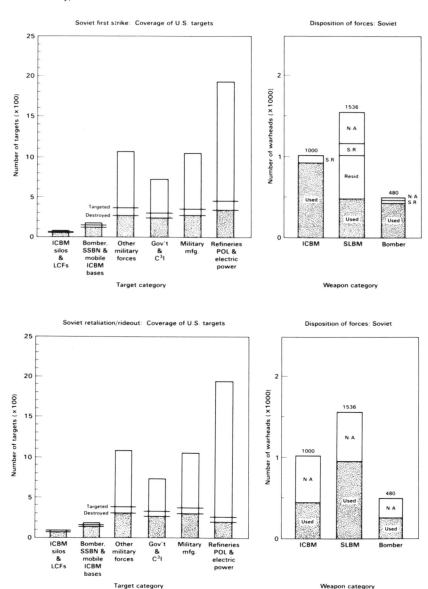

FIGURE 23. **Exchange simulations: Case F—Modernized forces (3,000 warheads), U.S. attacks**

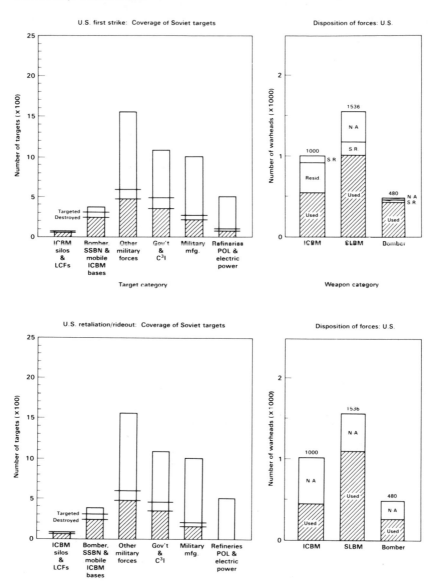

the Soviets retain a mix of mobile and silo-based ICBMs. Both the Soviet first strike and retaliation have target coverage essentially the same as that in the baseline case. There is a 10 percent strategic reserve plus residual forces in first strike, but no reserve at all after retaliation. U.S. target coverage is also equal to the baseline in first strike and retaliation, and because of the assumed high proportion of survivable forces, there are both a strategic reserve and residual forces for both attacks.

Figures 16 and 17 for case C illustrate results for 6,000 warheads with a modernized mixture of mobile and silo-based forces. The comments above for case B apply about as well to case C. Target coverage is as good as the baseline for all attacks. Again, because of the assumed superior survivability of U.S. forces, they have better strategic reserves and residual forces after the retaliatory attacks.

Figures 18 and 19 illustrate case D, which is for 3,000 warheads proportionally reduced from case A. For both Soviet and U.S. first strikes, target coverage is equal to baseline coverage and the 10 percent (300 warhead) strategic reserve is retained. There are no surplus or residual forces. For the retaliatory attacks in this case, coverage of the lower-priority targets falls off for both countries, and there are no strategic reserves.

Figures 20 and 21 are for case E. This 3,000-warhead case assumes maximum mobility for both sides, each having 1,000 mobile ICBMs. The forces are very symmetrical. Target coverage in first strike and retaliation is essentially identical for both sides and equal to the baseline. Strategic reserves are attained in each situation, and there are even small residual forces after the retaliatory attacks.

Figures 22 and 23 illustrate case F. This 3,000-warhead case incorporates a mix of forces similar to case C at 6,000 warheads. Like the case E results, the forces of the two sides in case F are very symmetrical. Target coverage in first strike is like the baseline, and there is a strategic reserve for both countries. For the retaliatory attacks, coverage falls off for the lowest-priority targets, and there are no reserves.

In summary, for the baseline case and the 6,000-warhead

cases A, B, and C, whether for first strike or retaliation scenarios, and whether launch under attack is used or not, there are enough weapons to cover most of the assumed target system, U.S. or Soviet, to much the same extent. Most of the differences between the cases are in the size of reserves and the residuals. For the United States, the differences that do exist in coverage and in reserves favor cases B and C over the baseline case and the case of proportional reductions, case A. The reason is the greater survivability of the modernized forces, especially case B (maximum mobility).

The simulation results for the baseline and 6,000-warhead cases are of course influenced by the assumptions we have made about weapons, target types and numbers, and the target coverage required for military effectiveness or deterrence. Nonetheless, the main features of the analysis should survive reasonable variations in the assumptions. The results should provide a point of departure for evaluating the effect of reducing forces to about 6,000 weapons.

For cases D, E, and F with 3,000 weapons, target coverage in first-strike scenarios, with allowance for reduced numbers of ICBMs, is essentially the same as for the baseline and 6,000-weapon cases for both sides. Coverage for the retaliation with rideout scenarios for both sides falls off for the lower-priority targets except for case E, the highest-survivability case. Ten percent strategic reserves are attained for all first strikes, but only case E has a reserve after retaliation.

Of all the cases analyzed, case D for both sides has the greatest loss of target coverage in retaliation with rideout. The exercise of a launch-under-attack option for this case would be expected to improve target coverage somewhat. Figures 24 and 25, for the Soviets and United States respectively, compare target coverage in first strike, retaliation with LUA, and retaliation with rideout for case D. (Case D was previously illustrated in figures 18 and 19 for first strike and rideout only.) Launch under attack goes some but not all the way toward restoring target coverage to the first-strike level in case D. There are still insufficient forces for a strategic reserve, however.

FIGURE 24. **Exchange simulations: Case D—Proportionally reduced forces (3,000 warheads), Soviet attacks, with launch under attack**

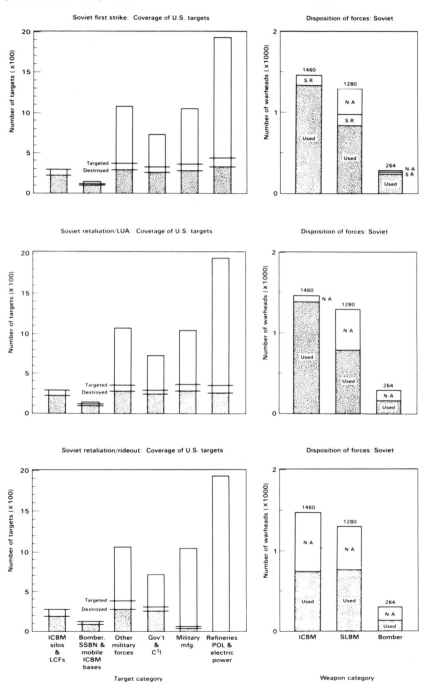

FIGURE 25. **Exchange simulations: Case D—Proportionally reduced forces (3,000 warheads), U.S. attacks, with launch under attack**

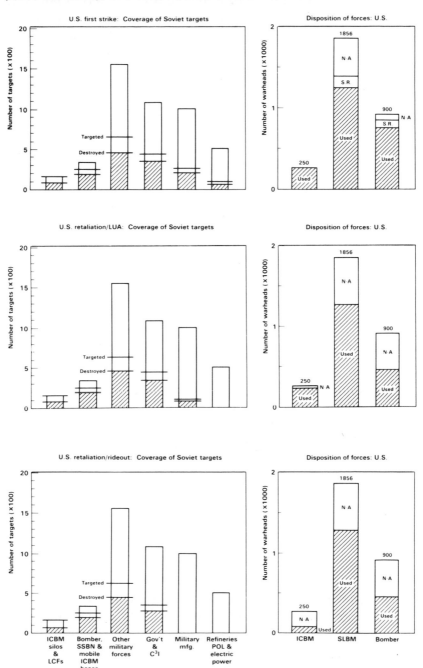

At this point, it may well be objected that a different targeting doctrine in retaliation—for instance, a doctrine of retaliating against civilian targets only, and of not trying to limit further damage from follow-on military action by the side striking first—could obviate these coverage problems at the lower force levels. Indeed, such a doctrine would imply fewer targets. The simulations suggest at what point, under the assumptions made, the assumed targeting doctrine can no longer be followed.

One can make some general comments for all the cases regarding the sensitivity of the results to the assumptions made about alert rates and vulnerability. As to bombers, U.S. bombers for current forces and our assumed reduced forces are assigned only about 20 percent to 30 percent of the strategic weapons, of which 33 percent to 50 percent are on day-to-day alert. Soviet bombers carry even fewer weapons. Accordingly, increasing the alert rate of bombers, an extremely expensive thing to do because of the associated logistical and personnel costs, would have only a modest effect on the available weapons and the simulation results.

We have assumed all bomber weapons to be cruise missiles, with high penetrativity. Credible variations in overall bomber and cruise missile penetration will have only small effects on the results of the simulations.

So long as a potential SLBM barrage threat exists, basing U.S. bombers inland is necessary if the survival of alert bombers is to be maintained. We have assumed all alert bombers are so based and effectively invulnerable.

SLBMs provide from 50 percent to 75 percent of the retaliatory weapons. The results of the simulations are therefore quite sensitive to both the assumption that submarines at sea are invulnerable and the assumed submarine alert rates. For the United States, the assumed rates can probably not be much further increased. For the Soviet Union, raising the alert rate from 30 percent to 60 percent would substantially increase their retaliatory capability.

For the cases that include single-warhead mobile ICBMs, we have assumed the alert missiles are not attacked by barrage or

TABLE 6. **Strategic reserve warheads and residual warheads**

| | | Reduced forces | | | | | |
| | | 6,000-warhead cases | | | 3,000-warhead cases | | |
Type of attack	Baseline	A	B	C	D	E	F
				SOVIET UNION			
First strike							
Strategic reserve	900	570	590	590	300	300	300
Residual	3,500	1,670	2,650	2,690	10	680	520
Retaliation—LUA							
Strategic reserve	1,000	570	600	600	0	a	270
Residual	490	370	160	80	0	a	0
Retaliation—rideout							
Strategic reserve	950	100	0	0	0	300	0
Residual	0	0	0	0	0	20	0
				UNITED STATES			
First strike							
Strategic reserve	1,000	600	600	600	230	300	300
Residual	2,560	1,260	2,180	2,400	0	520	380
Retaliation—LUA							
Strategic reserve	1,000	590	a	600	0	a	280
Residual	460	0	a	630	0	a	0
Retaliation—rideout							
Strategic reserve	870	570	600	600	0	300	0
Residual	0	0	480	190	0	50	0

a. No launch under attack.

other means, since the number of attacking warheads would be prohibitively large. The mobile missiles are thus assumed effectively invulnerable. For cases B and E, in particular, where mobile missiles represent a large fraction of the alert forces, this is a key assumption. Just how reasonable the assumption of invulnerability is would depend on actual operational deployment modes of mobile missiles and individual missile hardness.

Table 6 provides a summary of the number of reserve and residual warheads for all the simulations, including retaliations with launch under attack. In general, the desired strategic reserve is about 10 percent of the total initial force in each case.

FIVE

Civil Damage

In our nuclear exchange simulations, no nonmilitary industries or population centers were included as targets for direct attack. Yet clearly attacks on military targets in and near cities will cause extensive casualties and damage to nearby buildings, industry, and facilities. The Arsenal Exchange Model (AEM) calculations we did to estimate target coverage did not provide any direct assessment of civilian effects. To obtain rough estimates of civil damage, primarily the number of deaths, we have combined the results on military target coverage from the AEM with some simple prescriptions for calculating these effects.

The AEM deals with target types. All the targets of a type are treated as identical. Our simulation results include the number of each target type destroyed and the number and yield of the weapons that have been used against them. We have divided all the target types into three groups, according to our estimate of the typical surrounding population densities. ICBM silo targets are all classed as rural; airfields, refineries, electric power stations, and so forth are considered to be of intermediate population density; and manufacturing targets are considered urban.

A nuclear explosion of a specific yield over a target will have lethal or damaging effects extending to some distance from the burst point. The larger the yield, the greater the distance a given effect extends. The circular area covered by lethal effects, multiplied by the average population density surrounding the target, gives a rough estimate of the civilian deaths produced by the burst.

Casualty rates (deaths plus severe and moderate injuries) from a nuclear explosion over a populated area will be very high, virtually 100 percent, beneath the burst, and decrease in a poorly known manner with increasing distance. Detailed studies of the casualties at Hiroshima and Nagasaki provide the principal empirical data on the variation of casualty rates with distance.[13] Deaths and injuries in Japan were caused in varying degrees and combinations by blast, thermal radiation, and nuclear radiation. Some casualties were the direct result of blast and radiation, while others were secondary consequences from effects such as building collapse, projectile impact, and fires ignited in part by the bomb's thermal radiation and in part by blast disruption of stoves, electrical connections, and so forth. The Hiroshima and Nagasaki casualty model has been used in most analyses of likely casualties in hypothetical nuclear wars.

The bomb yield at Hiroshima was 15 kilotons and at Nagasaki 22 kilotons. To apply the observed casualty rates to other nuclear weapon yields requires a judgment on how casualty rates versus distance scale with weapon yield. Scaling by the cube root of the yield has been the standard method, equivalent to assuming that, for any yield explosion, the casualty rates will be the same as in Japan at the distance where the peak blast overpressure is the same. For example, the 15-kiloton Hiroshima explosion gave a fatality rate of about 30 percent at a distance of one mile from the burst point, and at that distance the peak overpressure was about 5 pounds per square inch (psi). A one-megaton airburst explosion would produce a 5-psi overpressure at about four miles, that is, the one-mile distance for the

13. Ashley W. Oughterson and Shields Warren, eds., *Medical Effects of the Atomic Bomb in Japan* (McGraw-Hill, 1956), pp. 23–71.

15-kiloton explosion multiplied by the cube root of the ratio of the yields, or $(1000/15)^{1/3} = 4.0$. Cube-root scaling of rates then means the fatality rate for a megaton explosion would be 30 percent at four miles.

But in fact for many years analysts have recognized that such cube-root scaling of casualty rates is not really satisfactory, especially for yields that are much greater than the nominal 20 kilotons used in Japan. The "mixture" of effects from blast and direct thermal radiation changes with yield: thermal effects increase relative to blast effects as yields increase. Unfortunately, the consequences, in terms of fire ignition, damage to buildings, and casualties, of this changing mixture of effects are not well understood or readily modeled. It is clear, however, that there would be more deaths at higher yields than those predicted on the basis of the Japanese experience.

For the basic fatality estimates made in this study, we have used the Japanese casualty rates scaled by the cube root of yield. We have further approximated the actual fatality rate distribution versus distance or overpressure by a model that assumes that everyone exposed to pressures greater than or equal to 5 psi is killed and that no one dies at lower pressures. There would, of course, be deaths at pressures less than 5 psi and survivors at pressures over 5 psi; we assume these would be about equal.

As an example of the application of this fatality model, a 100-kiloton weapon exploded at 4,500 feet would produce over-pressures of more than 5 psi out to about two miles, and an area of twelve square miles would be subjected to immediate lethal effects. For a target in an area with 4,000 persons per square mile, a reasonable average for the United States urban density, some 48,000 people would be killed. To estimate total civilian deaths in an attack, one must repeat the calculation for each combination of target type attacked, weapon yield, and population density, and add up the results.

Consider a Soviet first strike against the United States with the baseline forces, roughly their current strategic forces. In the attack simulation, the Soviets are assumed to deliver about 3,700 weapons with a total yield of 1,500 megatons against some 2,150 targets in the United States. Nine hundred of the targets, mostly ICBM silos and launch control facilities, are in rural areas, and they are struck by 2,450 weapons with a total yield of 870 megatons. Eight hundred targets in areas of intermediate population density are destroyed by 830 weapons with a total yield of 440 megatons. Finally, 450 targets in urban areas are destroyed by 460 weapons with a total yield of 190 megatons. We assume that, for the United States, the average population density for rural targets is 10 persons per square mile, for intermediate density areas, 750, and for urban areas, 4,000.[14] Assuming that *all* people subjected to 5 psi or greater overpressure are killed, there would be 0.3 million rural, 20 million intermediate, and 47 million urban deaths, for a total of about 67 million prompt fatalities.

This estimating procedure clearly has significant uncertainties. We have briefly discussed the fact that the Japanese casualty rate versus distance data scaled to higher yields may lead to underestimates of deaths. Recently, Postol has attempted to model the casualty rates at higher yields by taking account of some possible effects inadequately represented in the standard fatality model.[15] His casualty model assumes that a megaton airburst explosion will cause an intense "superfire" to develop and spread very rapidly out to a radius of about twelve kilometers (seven and a half miles), and that everyone within this region will be killed. This fire area is more than three times the lethal area predicted by the Japanese casualty rate model. Postol himself notes the substantial uncertainties in his model; it almost certainly represents an upper limit on prompt-fatality prediction models.

14. Authors' estimates based on U.S. Bureau of the Census, *County and City Data Book, 1983* (GPO, 1983); and William Daugherty, Barbara Levi, and Frank von Hippel, "The Consequences of 'Limited' Nuclear Attacks on the United States," *International Security*, vol. 10 (Spring 1986), pp. 3–45.

15. Theodore A. Postol, "Possible Fatalities from Superfires following Nuclear Attacks in or near Urban Areas," in Frederic Solomon and Robert Q. Marston, eds., *The Medical Implications of Nuclear War* (Washington, D.C.: National Academy Press, 1986), pp. 15–72.

Daugherty, Levi, and von Hippel have used a slightly modified version of Postol's model to estimate an upper limit on casualties in attacks on the United States.[16] For a megaton explosion, they assume everyone is killed out to ten kilometers and 50 percent are killed from ten to twelve kilometers. This model gives three times the deaths predicted by the standard model at one megaton. In a study of an attack on the Soviet Union, they assume the fatality radius scales as the yield to the 0.42 power.[17] At a yield of about 300 kilotons, their model would give about twice the standard fatality prediction. All these comparisons of fatality-model predictions assume a uniform density distribution of population over the entire area of the effects.

We do not present detailed fatality estimates based on the fatality-rate models of Postol or Daugherty, Levi, and von Hippel in this study. We believe use of either model would overestimate fatalities. As an approximation to the number of deaths that would be predicted by those models for the yield distributions in our exchange scenarios, one can double the predictions of prompt deaths presented in tables 7 and 8 below. (Yields used in urban target attacks for our simulations typically average about 300 kilotons or less.)

The assumption that population densities can be represented by single values for rural, intermediate, and urban areas is uncertain by at least plus or minus 25 percent. The choice of urban population density is the most critical for our simulations, since more than 70 percent of all fatalities are associated with targets in urban areas.

Many cities will contain several targets. For our fatality estimates, we have assumed all targets are far enough apart so that there is no overlap of lethal areas. This assumption almost certainly leads to counting some deaths twice and thus to an overestimate. The overestimation would be proportionately

16. Daugherty and others, "Consequences of 'Limited' Nuclear Attacks," pp. 5, 13–15.

17. Barbara G. Levi, Frank N. von Hippel, and William H. Daugherty, "Civilian Casualties from 'Limited' Nuclear Attacks on the Soviet Union," *International Security*, vol. 12 (Winter 1987–88), p. 170.

greater if a larger lethal area criterion, such as those discussed above, were used instead of the 5-psi area criterion.

An important question is how deaths might change under different force levels and mixtures. The relative values should be reasonably predicted by our calculations. Whatever the uncertainties in our assumptions, the choices have been used consistently for all fatality estimates.

In addition to immediate deaths, there would also be injured people, many requiring care for burns, traumatic injuries, and radiation exposure. Because medical care facilities would be very limited, their fate would be highly uncertain. At Hiroshima and Nagasaki about as many people were injured as were killed. We have not made a specific estimate of the injured for this analysis. They would about equal the dead if the Japanese casualty-rate model were used. If Postol's "superfire" model were used, the fraction of injured would decrease, since many injured people would be killed by fire.

Besides estimating prompt casualties from blast and fire, some evaluation of fallout casualties is necessary. Only nuclear explosions that burst on or near the surface produce significant local fallout. We have assumed that only attacks on ICBM silos and launch control facilities are groundbursts. Because these targets are all in lightly populated areas, fallout becomes significant, relative to prompt casualties, only if the winds carry lethal fallout levels to more populous areas. We have no specific fallout calculations for our simulations. Instead, we have used data from published studies by others to make rough guesses at fallout deaths for our several cases.[18] The total radioactive material available for producing fallout is proportional to the total fission yield of the groundburst weapons. For our simu-

18. Department of Defense, "Sensitivity of Collateral Damage to Limited Nuclear War Scenarios," *Analyses of Effects of Limited Nuclear Warfare*, Committee Print, Subcommittee on Arms Control, International Organizations and Security Agreements of the Senate Committee on Foreign Relations, 94 Cong. 1 sess. (GPO, 1975), p. 14; U.S. Congress, Office of Technology Assessment, *The Effects of Nuclear War* (GPO, 1979); Ted Harvey, Lawrence Livermore National Laboratory, personal communication; and fallout analyses in Daugherty and others, "Consequences of 'Limited' Nuclear Attacks," and Levi and others, "Civilian Casualties from 'Limited' Nuclear Attacks."

lations the total yield in groundbursts ranges from 1,000 mega-tons for the baseline case to zero for cases with no silo-based missiles (cases B and E).

Fallout deaths depend on the radiation levels in populated areas, the degree of shielding (the "protection factor") available and used in the exposed areas, and the amount of radiation required to kill people. For our fallout fatality estimates, we assume the average protection factor is about five, and that a radiation dose of 450 rads will kill 50 percent of those receiving it.[19]

Fallout deaths are greatest for the first-strike baseline cases. A Soviet first strike on U.S. ICBM fields (about 800 megatons, all weapons groundburst) is estimated to lead to between 2 million and 6 million fallout deaths, depending on the wind patterns. A U.S. first strike on Soviet missile fields with about 1,000 megatons groundburst is very roughly estimated at 8 million fallout deaths. Because the reduced-force cases posit fewer hard targets than the baseline cases do, attacking them requires a smaller total yield, producing substantially less fallout. The estimated fallout deaths for these cases are typically a million or less.

Tables 7 and 8 summarize the estimated deaths for our seven force cases. Note that Soviet urban population density has been taken to be 9,300 persons per square mile, more than twice the 4,000 assumed for the United States.[20]

We believe that these fatality estimates for the war scenario assumptions we have made are on the low side. Even for the

19. See, for example, OTA, *Effects of Nuclear War*, p. 19; Samuel Glasstone and Philip J. Dolan, *The Effects of Nuclear Weapons*, 3d ed. (GPO, 1977), pp. 575–87; and for a different view, see Joseph Rotblat, "Acute Radiation Mortality in a Nuclear War," in Solomon and Marston, eds., *Medical Implications of Nuclear War*, pp. 233–50.

20. For data on Soviet population distribution, see G. Melvyn Howe, *The Soviet Union: A Geographical Study*, 2d ed. (Estover, England: Macdonald and Evans, 1983); Geoffrey Kemp, *Nuclear Forces for Medium Powers*, pt. 1: *Targets and Weapons Systems*, Adelphi Paper 106, and pts. 2 and 3: *Strategic Requirements and Options*, Adelphi Paper 107 (London: International Institute for Strategic Studies, 1974); R. A. French, "The Individuality of the Soviet City," in French and F. E. Ian Hamilton, eds., *The Socialist City: Spatial Structure and Urban Policy* (New York: John Wiley & Sons, 1979), pp. 73–104; and J. C. Dewdney, *USSR in Maps* (New York: Holmes and Meier, 1982), pp. 28–37.

TABLE 7. **Estimated U.S. deaths from Soviet attacks**

Simulation case[a]	Yield delivered (megatons)		Prompt deaths[b] (millions)				Fallout deaths (millions)
	Airburst	Total	Urban	Inter-mediate	Rural	Total	
Baseline							
First strike	670	1,500	47	20	0.3	67	2.0–6.0
Retaliation	660	890	56	21	0.2	77	0.6–1.6
Case A							
First strike	470	870	48	15	0.2	63	1.0–3.0
Retaliation	460	530	48	15	0.1	63	0.2–1.5
Case B							
First strike	520	520	42	16	0.1	58	0
Retaliation	420	420	28	13	0.1	41	0
Case C							
First strike	510	560	43	18	0.1	61	0.1–0.3
Retaliation	390	440	38	12	0.1	50	0.1–0.3
Case D							
First strike	220	460	20	9	0.1	29	0.6–1.6
Retaliation	75	280	7	4	0.1	11	0.5–1.4
Case E							
First strike	330	330	28	13	0.1	41	0
Retaliation	330	330	27	11	0	38	0
Case F							
First strike	320	390	26	12	0.1	39	0.2–0.4
Retaliation	200	270	22	7	0.1	29	0.2–0.4

a. The cases termed "retaliation" refer to U.S. deaths from Soviet retaliatory attacks by forces surviving a U.S. first strike.

b. Assumed population densities in the United States are: urban, 4,000 persons per square mile; intermediate, 750 persons per square mile; and rural, 10 persons per square mile. See text note 14.

lowest totals, however, there are more than 10 million deaths. In general, total deaths from first strikes are comparable to those from retaliatory strikes after riding out an attack because attacks on targets in urban areas account for most fatalities, and coverage of such targets is essentially always possible in both first strike and retaliation. According to our very rough estimates, fallout deaths are, with one exception, less than 10 percent of prompt fatalities.

The prompt-fatality predictions in the Soviet Union for cases C and F, table 8, are approximately twice those for the other cases in the table. This result follows from one specific assumption made for the U.S. forces in these cases, namely, that all U.S. Trident submarines are equipped with the D-5 missile

TABLE 8. **Estimated Soviet deaths from U.S. attacks**

Simulation case[a]	Yield delivered (megatons)		Prompt deaths[b] (millions)				Fallout deaths (millions)
	Airburst	Total	Urban	Inter- mediate	Rural	Total	
Baseline							
First strike	250	1,240	37	8	0.9	46	8.0
Retaliation	150	480	27	5	0.4	32	3.0
Case A							
First strike	240	615	36	7	0.4	43	3.0
Retaliation	180	220	27	6	0.2	33	0.4
Case B							
First strike	300	440	37	9	0.2	46	2.0
Retaliation	260	320	37	8	0.3	45	1.0
Case C							
First strike	690	780	91	15	0.2	106	0.1
Retaliation	600	680	61	15	0.2	76	0.1
Case D							
First strike	160	400	26	6	0.1	32	0.3
Retaliation	110	190	7	5	0.1	12	0.1
Case E							
First strike	290	290	36	9	0.1	45	0
Retaliation	250	250	33	8	0.1	41	0
Case F							
First strike	470	530	80	11	0.1	91	0.1
Retaliation	450	510	55	11	0.1	66	0.1

a. The cases termed "retaliation" refer to Soviet deaths from U.S. retaliatory attacks by forces surviving a Soviet first strike.

b. Assumed population densities in the Soviet Union are: urban, 9,300 persons per square mile; intermediate, 500 persons per square mile; and rural, 25 for baseline and cases A and C, 10 for cases B, D, E, and F. See text note 20.

having a higher-yield warhead compared with the C-4 missile.[21] Submarine-launched warheads account for a large fraction of the weapons used against urban targets both in first strike and retaliation. The assumed yield of almost half a megaton, compared with the assumed 100-kiloton warheads for Poseidon and Trident C-4 missiles, accounts for the approximate doubling of fatalities.

In general, the high yield of the D-5 warhead would not be needed to destroy the targets we have assumed to be in urban areas. The sensitivity of fatality estimates to the number of targets attacked in or near urban areas points up the fact that

21. See, for example, CBO, *Modernizing*; IISS, *Military Balance 1985–1986*; and Cochran and others, *Nuclear Weapons Databook*.

withholding attacks on such targets or using lower-yield accurate weapons could do much to reduce immediate deaths.

We have not estimated damage to nonmilitary facilities caused by attacks on military targets. The most important of those facilities are in urban areas. They are typically "soft" structures that would be badly damaged by overpressures of about 5 psi and would be subject to fire besides. Plainly the nuclear exchanges described in our simulations would wreak tremendous damage on the civil industry and economies of both nations.

Nor have we taken account of possible civil defense measures in estimating casualties. Evacuating urban areas and providing shelter could, in principle, reduce deaths substantially, but we have not tried to quantify the benefits or determine how elaborate the measures would have to be.[22]

22. U.S. Arms Control and Disarmament Agency, *An Analysis of Civil Defense in Nuclear War* (Washington, D.C.: ACDA, 1978); Director of Central Intelligence, *Soviet Civil Defense*, CIA Report NI78-10003 (Washington, D.C., 1978). See also Sidney D. Drell, Eugene P. Wigner, and Arthur A. Broyles, "Civil Defense in Limited War—A Debate," *Physics Today*, vol. 29 (April 1976), pp. 44–57.

SIX

Conclusion

In this study, we have examined the effects of various U.S. and Soviet strategic force configurations of 10,000, 6,000, and 3,000 weapons each, as to:

—their effectiveness against each other (drawdowns) in a first strike, with and without launch under attack;

—their effectiveness, in a first strike and in retaliation, against a broader set of targets, constituting the bulk of each side's ability to wage or continue the war;

—very approximately, the deaths that might result from some of these nuclear exchanges.

At present levels of forces, roughly 10,000 strategic warheads on each side, mutual deterrence is assured. Cutting forces by half does not seem to introduce any serious departure from this situation, insofar as these simulations can represent it, provided that attention is paid to the survivability of the remaining components. In fact, if forces are modernized to increase the survivability of ICBMs, better target coverage can be attained after absorbing a first strike.

For reductions below 6,000 warheads, the survivability and alert rates of the forces become more and more important if a

70

disarming first strike is to remain an impossibility and if there are to be enough residual forces to carry out the specified military missions and maintain reserves. The simulations cannot give a precise level that will correlate with some military capability. There are too many unresolvable unknowns in attempting to predict the outcome of nuclear exchanges to permit more than rough estimates of qualitative trends. As one departs more and more from the present situation, calculations become less and less trustworthy in analyzing the consequences of reductions, and the element of judgment, more and more important.

Improving survivability and day-to-day alert rates is a costly and time-consuming objective. New systems and new ways of fielding existing systems must be developed and tested. Reduction in overall force levels should free up some funds, but, in addition, time must be allowed in the transition to lower levels of forces for both sides to do this developing and testing if a secure deterrent balance at lower levels of force is the goal. The two sides have different problems and probably also quite different perceptions of these problems. A careful study of these aspects of the transition is needed, particularly in connection with the negotiation of such details of reductions as extent, sublimitations, and schedules.

If offensive forces were reduced to the point where large sets of targets could not be covered in retaliation and a retaliatory strike would not necessarily prevent the attacker from continuing the war, even though large damage had been done to its country, then cheating and the ability to rebuild forces rapidly in a crisis could become important. It now makes little difference whether more forces are built or not, so there is little incentive for either cheating or maintaining the capability to build more forces rapidly. Both, however, become potentially important if a real strategic advantage could be attained by adding forces, and some insurance against cheating and rapid buildup would be needed. Such insurance could take the form of effective defenses, or of enforceable assurances that other forces did not exist and additional forces could not be built promptly, or both.

The latter would require much more severe verification and enforcement than arms control treaties to date have yet envisaged. The former may or may not be possible or desirable on other counts.

No examination of the effect of defenses has been carried out in this study. Introducing defense raises, first of all, the question whether the eventual goal is to continue relying on offensive deterrence or to replace it with some other method of averting war and the conditions that lead to war. If offensive deterrence is to be relied on, either for a time or indefinitely, then introducing defenses raises questions of stability.[23]

Within the calculus of weapon exchanges considered in our analysis, partially effective defenses would be equivalent to cuts in the offense of uncertain effectiveness (uncertain, both to the side introducing the defense and to its opponent). Mathematically, one could presumably assess these uncertain cuts by weighting the results obtained here with some probability function representing the possible outcomes of an engagement between defense and offense. The uncertainties in both our work and the probability function are such that only the simplest qualitative conclusions could be drawn. It seems likely that defense, like reductions, would make the survivability of offensive systems even more important than it is now if the first-strike advantage is to be minimized.

Introducing defenses would demand a broader assessment, however, and would raise many military, strategic, and political questions. For example, the defense sites, in space and on the ground, are new targets that must be taken into account in modeling the results of exchanges. The survivability of these sites may affect the survivability of command and control functions, which we have assumed to be survivable in this work. The entire process of defense and launch could be more complex and drawn out in time than without defenses. Penetration prospects might be substantially different for an initiating

---

23. Claire E. Max and others, *Deployment Stability of Strategic Defenses*, JASON Report JSR-85-926 (McLean, Va.: Mitre Corp., 1986).

attack than for a retaliatory one. Preferential defense might play a major role.[24]

Sufficiently deep reductions in strategic offensive forces on the part of the United States and the Soviet Union, whether or not accompanied by the introduction of defenses, could make other forces, conventional as well as nuclear, strategically and politically more important. It is hard to foresee the likely long-term reaction of the major U.S. allies to a situation where the United States would no longer be so obviously the militarily and strategically dominant partner. National considerations might become more important than alliance considerations. Such an effect would not be expected in the case of the Soviet Union and the Warsaw Pact. Equally important in the long run would be the reaction of China to such an altered state of affairs.

We do not in this study discuss these and other considerations that could attend deep reductions in offense, with or without defenses. Reductions in nuclear arms would be, as the buildup was, a highly political affair, the desirability of which cannot be completely assessed on the basis of descriptions of exchanges at reduced force levels. But descriptions such as those in this study can and should set out the boundaries for the debate.

24. Michael M. May, "Safeguarding Our Space Assets," in Joseph S. Nye, Jr., and James A. Schear, eds., *Seeking Stability in Space: Anti-Satellite Weapons and the Evolving Space Regime* (Lanham, Md.: Aspen Strategy Group and University Press of America, 1987), pp. 71–85.